The Black Sheep of the Blue Family

OLIVE ELISE

ISBN 979-8-89112-032-7 (Paperback)
ISBN 979-8-89112-033-4 (Digital)

First Edition

Covenant Books
11661 Hwy 707
Murrells Inlet, SC 29576
www.covenantbooks.com

ACKNOWLEDGMENTS

First and foremost, I would like to dedicate this book to God. Even through the difficult times in life, He has always been my safety and hope. I would not be here today without Him.

I would also like to dedicate this book to my immediate family and to my very close friends (you know who you are) who have believed in me and loved me throughout every step of this journey.

To all the women in law enforcement—past, present, and future.

And finally, to the one person who helped me find my voice after this trauma, my sergeant. *You* made the difference for me when nobody else would.

READER DISCRETION ADVISED

While the chapters in these pages are very raw and tough to read, please know that I have found healing. It has not been easy and has been quite a long process that I must work every day to overcome so the triggers do not overtake or overwhelm me. I will likely have to work for the rest of my life to maintain that healing. Yet God has been gracious to pull me out of the pit of despair and lead me into His marvelous light once again. He can do the same for you because He loves you *so* much! Perhaps you, too, can find healing through my story.

As you read through the following pages, please know that it is not formatted in chronological order of how I wrote it initially nor how I have felt throughout this trauma journey. The manuscript goes back and forth between journal entries and chapters, because through the difficult times, I am trying to convey that God is still good. Sometimes the pages may seem like a jumbled mess, because trauma gets messy.

My journal entries were written *during* this trauma and came from a place of deep pain while trying to understand the purpose behind it. The chapters within this book were then written several years later as my way, and God's way, of working out my faith with fear and trembling (Philippians 2:12–13), because I could not stay mad at God forever. While it felt as such, He did not make this happen to me. God has done a great work in my heart, and together we have made it out of the wilderness of sorrow, which is hopefully reflected throughout the next pages.

If you or a loved one has experienced sexual assault, please seek out help. Healing will not come without it. You are so worth it!

For more information, additional resources, or to find help near you, please visit the Rape, Abuse & Incest National Network (RAINN) at www.rainn.org.

Due to the possible triggering nature of this manuscript, reader discretion is advised.

Journal Entry
I Am Her

Several years ago, there was an article published about a female police officer that was sexually assaulted by her superior officer. I will not reveal the case name for safety reasons, nor will I reveal that agency or supervisor's name.

I am her. I am that female officer.

And I was silenced by them.

I wish that I was strong enough back then to share my story, but I refrained because I was filled with fear, not only from the assaults that took place against my body but also from the direct retaliation I faced by my department for speaking up. Sadly, retaliation is what happens when someone speaks up.

While the details of my case shall remain undisclosed out of respect for my privacy and dignity, both which were stolen away from me throughout this battle, I would like to have my voice heard now, to share my perspective as a female officer for the future safety of all women who dare to bravely put on a uniform as a first responder.

I loved my career as a law enforcement officer. Although short-lived, as I was forced to resign because of this nightmare, I still strived to make a difference for the community I served. Now I long to make a difference for the women who are still living out my first responder dream.

Law enforcement was my dream. It was taken from me by the corrupt politics of a broken system. I cannot get it back again because my name seems to be forever highlighted as a disgrace to the department because I fought back. I am the black sheep of the blue family.

Although there is a very negative stigma surrounding officers today, not all of them are bad. Most truly do desire to protect and serve their communities. I had the distinct privilege of working with many fine officers. I still know many wonderful police officers today. Yet there does not seem to be much protection for the women behind the badge when they are faced with hostility and harassment from their own team. My story is proof of that.

Unfortunately, I am not the only female to face severe sexual harassment, sexual assault, and/or backlash while in my uniform. I am very likely one of hundreds, maybe even thousands, of women across the country. It seems there are media stories about this happening frequently within the United States.

If we could gather female first responders together and give them the opportunity to share about what they have faced within their positions, we would then learn a lot about the problem and then try to work together to find a proper solution. Sadly, however, many will never be able to speak up because it could risk their safety within their jobs.

The harassment was not usually from the community. It was from my own brothers in blue—because I was a female. I was not just hurt by one officer. Sexual harassment is a culture within the first-response career field, especially for women. It is very damaging mentally, emotionally, and physically.

Change is so desperately needed for women enduring this treatment because of the career they chose. Instead of facing harm and hatred from the department, we should be protected and believed when we report the negative behaviors of other officers. We should not be made to feel that we will face trouble or even possibly lose our jobs if we speak up. This is why I remained silent, scared, and suffering alone with this huge secret trauma because I knew I would not be safe if I talked because of who the assailant was.

We should be provided a safe space in which to be heard and not quickly turned away and rejected simply because the harassment and/or assault was done by a tenured officer with a high rank. We should be offered a completely fair and unbiased investigation, completed by another department in another county, a county that does not know the involved parties whatsoever.

We should never be automatically labeled as just another "adulterous female" because we are a first responder. We should not have to feel afraid to go to work every day because of the trouble we will face because of what is happening to us.

We should never feel that we are left to fight alone. We should not feel like we must prove what is happening because nobody else cared to believe us or to even listen to our deepest plea. We should not face losing our jobs because we choose to speak up about these atrocities in the department. Our stories should never be swept under the rug to protect the corruption. There should be zero tolerance instead of a complete allowance for the ongoing and harassing behaviors that have been reported by many, even years before we were sworn in.

I was not protected simply because of the power that one male officer held. The all-male command staff listened to his side of the story and believed it as truth but turned a deaf ear and a blind eye to mine.

He was well liked by his close friends in the command staff and many others. Yet he also had a reputation regarding his voluptuous behaviors with females, which was also widely known around the department. Everyone just seemed to accept that behavior, stating it was just "how he was."

I feel it is necessary to discuss just how deep the wanton and sensuous corruption goes within a first-response agency, not to tear them down but so it can safely and appropriately be built back up the right way once again.

It is not just one police officer, firefighter, paramedic, corrections officer, etc. It is many others also contributing to the negative culture for women in the first responder field. It seems it is a system that shames the victim. They keep the problem and terminate anyone who dares to speak out against it. This behavior does not affect just my former agency but many of them around this country, because this is a widely known and grievously accepted systemic issue.

Corruption begets corruption.

It starts by being covered up and silenced. Then it gets promoted. Then repeated.

How many females must get hurt, physically, mentally, and/or emotionally, before change is made? How many must lose their job because they finally say, "Enough is enough," and either leave in disgust or are forced out because they stood up against the harassment and hostile work environment? Yes, we made the decision to join a traditionally male-dominant career field, but we should not be subjected to negative behaviors just because we are female.

This is not just a first responder issue. This problem runs deep all the way through our cities and states and well into the government. Inappropriate behavior among our leaders is widely known yet vastly underreported because unfortunately, the good people are not able to or allowed to stand up to evil and corruption because it is so deep. When do we get justice?

#MeToo became a movement several years ago, but it seems that unless you have money or fame behind you, your story does not seem to really matter because sexual harassment and sexual assault still runs rampant in this country with very few stories being shared.

It was repeatedly proven that my life and struggles did not matter to my assailant. Neither to the state attorney nor to my own department. I was silenced by all of them. My story went unheard because #MeToo does not seem to apply to those without status or name recognition in this country.

Yes, I am her. I am that victim, that survivor that tried to fight against the injustice I faced behind the badge. As hard as I tried, I lost on several fronts because they believed his "truth," even though they quietly knew that I was actually telling the truth all along.

Many of those involved in my story still wear the uniform today. The high-ranking officer in my case was allowed to retire with a full pension. He can get back into law enforcement if he so chooses. And for me? Well, law enforcement is over for me because I was marked by the system as being the problem. Not the sexual harassment. Not the corruption. Not the assailant or even the sexual assault. I was marked for trying to speak up against it because it happened to me. Therein lies the problem.

Where is the justice? Where is the justice for all the women in first response who still face this culture today? Change is absolutely needed, but who is willing to step up and fight for this change?

I am her, but I am not silenced any longer. Please do not ever forget my name, my story, for all the women who are brave enough to put on that uniform every day.

We are her. We have a name. We have a story behind our uniforms. See the need and be the change for all female first responders everywhere.

CHAPTER 1

The facts are startling, daunting, heartbreaking, eye-opening. Almost too much to fathom. Yet they speak loud and clear as to just one of the many silent issues the world is facing today. When will the madness end? How many innocent people must become victims before it does? No means no!

By its very definition, the word *rape* means: "*(1) unlawful sexual intercourse or any other sexual penetration of the vagina, anus, or mouth of another person, with or without force, by a sex organ, other body part, or foreign object, without the consent of the victim; (2) an outrageous violation; (3) an act of plunder, violent seizure, or abuse; despoliation; violation*" (Dictionary.com).

In technical terms, the word *rape* does not actually exist in some statutes but is known by its legal term as *sexual battery*.

For example, many state statutes define *sexual battery* as being "*oral, anal, or vaginal penetration by, or in union with, the sexual organ of another or the anal or vaginal penetration of another by any object.*" Further statute reads, "*A person who commits sexual battery upon another person without that person's consent, commits a felony of the first degree.*" This is the pretty standard definition in most states.

Both sources are clear—*without consent*! No means no! Rape is *not* a game! It is a serious felony crime!

Now where were we? Ah, yes, the facts. The outrageous and horrific facts of the matter. Statistics do not lie. These statistics can be located on the Rape, Abuse & Incest National Network (RAINN) website.

Each year in the United States, there is an average of 433,648 people who are raped. (The numbers would increase significantly if the statistics were documented worldwide.) That means a rape occurs approximately every sixty-eight seconds. One in six women will experience a sexual assault/rape in her lifetime. Approximately one in every thirty-three men will experience one too. Out of every ten rapes that occur, nine of those victims are female.

The numbers do not stop there.

In America alone, most sexual crimes are *never* reported to law enforcement officials, which makes sexual battery (rape) the most underreported crime in the country. The average age of a victim is between twelve to thirty-four years of age.

Overwhelmed yet?

Approximately eight out of ten assaults are committed by someone known to the victim. Statistics show that 82 percent of victims reported knowing their assailant while only 18 percent reported the rapist to be a stranger.

The numbers are harrowing!

The average rape occurs *in* the home or within one mile from the home. Eighty-nine percent of victims report the rape as being completed with only physical force and not with a weapon at all.

Around 94 percent of victims experience post-traumatic stress disorder within two weeks of the assault, and 30 percent nine months afterward. PTSD can include chronic nightmares, eating disorders, substance abuse, severe depression, anxiety, and suicidal ideations or attempts. Additionally, 33 percent of female victims contemplate suicide, while 13 percent attempt it. About 70 percent of victims experience moderate to severe distress, which makes this worse than any other violent crime.

No means no!

The harshest reality for a rape victim is that most rapists will *never* spend a day in jail. Out of every 1,000 rapes, only 310 are reported to law enforcement. Only 50 will lead to an arrest. Only 28 will lead to a felony conviction. Only 25 perpetrators will be incarcerated. Out of 1,000 rapes, 975 rapists will walk free. Most rapists *are repeat offenders*.

It is a vicious cycle! An unfair reality for every victim!

Many people will never understand a true rape. They may gasp deeply at the sound of the word, or even feel overwhelmed while reading the statistics of such a crime, but they will never understand the actual implications of the action.

The surrounding world will never completely understand the life a victim has to live even after the painful minutes when the rape is over. They will likely never hear of the agonizing moments of being roughly penetrated anally, vaginally, and/or orally, all while their deepest pleas to stop go ignored.

They will never comprehend the true courage it takes to talk to the police about the heinous crime that has just been committed against their body and their soul. They will never be able to grasp the shame of having the painful rape kit done, which, in some cases, is like revictimizing the victim. They will never realize the fear and anguish that rips through the victim's soul in the days, weeks, and years to follow. They will not be able to perceive why the rape victim just cannot get out of bed or why they refuse to anyway. They will not understand the constant nightmares of the attack that seem to play on repeat throughout the victim's dreams, night after night, for years.

They will not know the fear each victim faces when they are finally able to resurface into reality. Is their rapist lurking in the shadows? Are they waiting to attack again? How can they trust society ever again? Ah, yes, the world will never truly know.

Unfortunately, many rape victims blame themselves for the rape, which is viewed as a coping mechanism. Some victims even form a *trauma bond* with their perpetrator, which leads them to shame and blame themselves for this crime. Even worse, in many cases, the victim's friends and family act in a judgmental manner. They act derisively and negatively toward them and blame them for the rape—sometimes without even realizing it.

No means no! No matter the situation or circumstances. Even within the very middle of intercourse, no means no.

How many more times do victims have to live in silence before this matter is resolved? How many times will the victim be revictimized because they were too afraid to speak up after the first occurrence? How many more victims does there have to be before 100 percent of offenders are held accountable for their actions?

The numbers speak loud and clear! No means no.

CHAPTER 2

I am not patient through the process of healing because of the shame left during the placement of the pain. Life is tough. From my earliest memories, it has been what seems to be one challenge after another. Knowing right from wrong is a basic skill learned at a young age, but living right instead of wrong can be a tough feat as you go, especially when dealing with trauma. I only know this because I have battled with this during different valleys in my life, because life is hard, and I did not like the placement of the pain.

So who needs forgiveness? God? Myself? Both? The very thing I have been learning over the years is that I need to learn to forgive God for my many hurts and letdowns that He "let" happen to me. I also need to forgive myself, too, for feeling the way I have been toward *me*. Toward God.

Now I do not believe that God purposefully does things to harm His beloved creations. That is not in His nature. Sin gleefully slips in and does that instead, with the help of our own weakness, of course. However, when life goes wrong, God is generally our first blame. Our own guilt, shame, and constant what-if questions from the situation tends to be our second.

When things go wrong, we usually blame those closest to us. So who is closer to us than God and our very own being? We need to learn to blame our fallen world and sinful nature when things go wrong. Not God. Yes, we should take responsibility for our part in the scenario, but living a daily life of reminiscent blaming and holding ourselves captive in a prison of our own making should not happen either.

Trauma causes broken people. Broken people tend to stay broken when they cannot accept what has happened enough to learn forgiveness and then to learn to move forward toward healing. Healing is difficult to achieve, especially with overly onerous baggage attached.

As hard as it seems, healing *is* possible because God is in the business of making all things new again (Revelation 21:5). He makes a way in the wilderness and a river in the desert (Isaiah 41:19). He makes the prison walls shake when we praise His name (Acts 16:16–40). Trusting is not always easy because just as the prison walls can shake, Satan has an innate ability to make us tremble in fear, too, when we let our guards down.

I have spent many years in the public safety and human services career field. The days are often long and filled with some form of vicarious trauma. I often relay to my clients, however, that even amid the sad, the *yuck* of life, there is still beauty nearby if we are willing to look for it.

The example I often share is that of a rainbow. Rainbows are colorful and vibrant. They bring smiles and joy to those who get to see one stretch across the sky during their day-to-day activities. The rainbow is a sign of God's promise (Genesis 9:13–16). So where does the rainbow come from? A storm cloud, perhaps? I have never been a witness to a rainbow that does *not* spring forth from a cloud.

The storms of life can be draining. Mentally. Physically. Emotionally. There is not always a positive outlook or a favorable outcome when in a battle. However, if we take the time to look, we can find the perfect amount of sunshine (Son-shine) in which to form a rainbow even when a storm is raging inside of us. Beauty *can* come from the ashes despite what the enemy (Satan) tries to make us believe.

So what do we do when there is no rainbow in the clouds or when there is no end in sight for our troubles? That is a question I have battled with for years now, because I struggle to trust that the God of the universe really does have everything under His control.

I fail to remember that He still loves me despite my past. I tend to forget that He will be my shield and portion as long as life endures (Psalm 142).

I overlook the fact that our light affliction is but for a moment (2 Corinthians 4:17–18). God will make us perfect. He will establish us. He will strengthen us. He will settle us after we have suffered a while (1 Peter 5:10). All things will eventually work together for our good if we love God and are called to His purpose (Romans 8:28). Yet I am not blind to the fact that trusting anyone, even God, is not always easy. What seems to be easy, however, is getting hurt because we live in a broken and fallen world.

Journal Entry

The Sheepdog: Who Will Fight for Us?

To quote the Holy Bible, "All we like sheep have gone astray; we have turned everyone to his own way..." (Isaiah 53:6a). We are all sheep. Some of us wear the mask of a sheepdog, but in the end, it is just a mask.

For a short time, I, too, proudly wore the mask of the sheepdog. I would prowl around the night and try to be strong for the weak. When I saw evil, I would growl and hiss ferociously, sometimes digging my teeth deep within, until the evil subsided. I walked around in this protective mode for those who could not help themselves.

Yes, I was a sheepdog. I was just one sheepdog in the pack—the pack of many who proudly bear the name law enforcement officer.

Being in our pack is no easy feat. You chase the worst of the worst because the world is evil. You respond to calls that no person should ever have to see. You see things play out before your very eyes that make you wonder if life is even worth it for anyone. You question with each shift how evil can be so prevalent. You wonder if you are going to make a difference, if you even can make a difference.

You arrest the same crackhead repeatedly. You show up to the same domestic disturbances where there is more blood on the floor than a blood bank sees in a day. You arrive at the car accident that has just taken the life of an innocent man because he happened to be in the wrong place at the wrong time—right next to the impaired driver.

You cradle the small child who has just breathed his last breath because his mother accidentally rolled on him in her sleep because of an endless number of drugs in her system. You carry the scared little toddler to the very arms of a relative as their father is being carted off to jail—for the sixth time, for the same reason.

You run toward the gunman not knowing exactly where he is located and if he wants to take vengeance out on you as you approach. You search the dark house that has just been raided by a burglar, hoping he is not still inside planning an attack. You hold tightly to the rape victim, not knowing exactly what she has just experienced but trying desperately to be her comfort.

You use your best words to coax the suicidal man from jumping off the bridge. You run to your area partner as he is in a fight for his life while attempting to detain a suspect who decided to pull a gun on him. You stop the car for another violation, praying they do not have a weapon pointed at you upon your approach. You run to the flames of a house fire that is overtaking the structure, hoping that nobody was left inside that you could not rescue.

You hear repeatedly, "I hope you get killed today!" simply because of the uniform you wear. You drive lights and sirens to the shots fired call, not knowing what your eyes will see upon arrival. You perform CPR on a woman that you beg God to save but that is eventually called as a "signal 7" (dead body) in the end. You listen carefully for your area partners and are there in a flash when they hit their emergency button.

Sometimes you shake a little inside, trying to keep yourself calm so as not to show your own fear. You fight away the adrenaline dump to continue working the scene where a life was just lost. While attending to another call, you sit and listen to the deadly motorcycle accident over your radio just before you learn that you were friends with the deceased victim.

You keep the crowds calm in utter chaos. You show the sheep that the sheepdog is there to take control. We are there to be a light in a dark world. We hold your hand and see you through your storm even if just for *the night. We cannot change you or your situation, but we will die trying. Ah, yes, we are the pack!*

At the end of the day, when our masks come off, who is there for us? We do not have the ability to turn a blind eye to the world when the badge comes off, and the gun is locked away. We always watch the hands of others. We constantly search with our eyes the people around us for bulges or weapons, questioning what their motives may be. We continuously scan our surroundings, wondering where the evil may be lurking—because it is lurking.

We lack empathy, sometimes even for another sheepdog, because of the evil that exists. We do not run and hide. We cannot. Yet who is there for us at the end of the day? Who is there during the painful hours where that one lonely sheepdog sits in his bedroom contemplating suicide with his own department-issued firearm? Who is there when the next sheepdog loses his marriage because of the stress of the job? Who is there as we cry our nights away because of that one call we just responded to that has taken our breath away? Who is there at the end of a career, whether it be one year or twenty, to hold close and encourage the sheepdog to see the bright side of the world? Who is there?

Everything is a fight in our pack. We fight the evil that exists in the world for others. We fight the defense in court. We fight our own fears, our own demons, which have a strong hold on us. We even fight against our own pack at times.

We fight because we must. We fight to win. We fight to live. We fight because we know no other way. Because remember, the sheepdog face we wear is just a mask. Who fights for us? Our family? Our friends who will never truly understand our battle? Our agency? Who? Am I not worth fighting for too?

Several years ago, I resigned from my position in the sheepdog pack. It was a heartbreaking decision that I did not have an option on in the end. I loved working with the agency and the people in it. From officers to civilians, it was truly a great place to work, to learn, to grow as an officer. Well, until I experienced the corruption for myself behind that badge. My heart breaks at just the mere thought of this unfortunate event. Who fights for me now?

As much as I would love to expose the evils of the typical police department, it is not going to win my job back. Perhaps I can shed some light on the issues we sheepdogs face within. When you go against the pack, you become the black sheep of the blue family.

A typical shift for me was to head in for squad meeting and be briefed on the happenings of the community. Each day was different. No shift was ever the same. I would then head out into the community to protect the place I cared about. My nights were long and busy, but I would have it no other way. I never enjoyed sitting idly, as settling for mediocrity was just not an option for me. I loved my job! I loved being a sheepdog in my pack! I enjoyed protecting my sheep.

I did well my first few months on the force. I excelled quickly and always strived for excellence! My record was nearly spotless. I truly enjoyed dressing up in my uniform and "going out to play" each day.

I eventually learned the mentality of the police department. It never bothered me to be a female in a male-dominated career. I guess I really did not know any better at the time. For that time, I enjoyed the constant camaraderie of the squad. I loved the brotherhood of the agency. I learned quickly who truly had my back and who would just sit and talk behind it to fit their own agenda. I learned to hold even the other sheepdogs at an arm's length.

There came a time in my short career where I faced what seemed to be an insurmountable challenge. I had been raped by another officer. I felt like I was facing Mount Everest knowing that I could not climb it alone. I struggled with this deeply personal issue that was caused by another sheepdog—a fellow sheepdog I thought I could trust. That sheepdog bit me in the end.

After I was raped, I began alienating myself from the other sheepdogs on the squad. I felt alone and abandoned. I felt betrayed and uncared for during my time of need. My demeanor began to change because something so personal was taken from me. I could not even tell my best friends of the matter.

One night, my sergeant came to me about the problem. He did not know what happened and probably only had his speculations. When questioned by him, I denied things and refused to speak of the matter. This was a matter that I had to deal with on my own because of who my assailant was. Furthermore, had I talked, someone would have gotten in trouble, and it likely would have been me.

For the next couple of weeks, I stayed quiet. I found myself hiding under the trees at the local park when the nights were slow. My proactivity decreased greatly. My bubbly personality dulled and became stale. Yet my sergeant kept gently prodding me for an answer. He reminded me that just because he had stripes on his sleeve did not mean that he was not my friend too. He spoke softly to me, encouraging me to speak of this incident that he knew had taken place.

After some time passed, I could not carry this burden by myself any longer. One night, after a lunch break with several other alpha male sheep-dogs, I confided in my sergeant. Because of the personal and sensitive nature of the matter, I begged him not to tell others, not yet at least.

In those moments, I did not see just a supervisor trying to pridefully carry out his role. I saw a person who truly cared for me in my circumstance. I saw a man who desired to go to battle for one of his sheepdogs because they were in trouble. From that point on, I did not just see another set of stripes on his sleeve. I saw a true leader in him. I saw a real concern from him, which was not the typical picture of any sheepdog within the agency. When I was in trouble, he stood up for me.

Following those nights, I began to take criticism and ridicule from the others on the squad. Rumors were spread that an inappropriate relationship was going on between that sergeant and me. It was advised that he was treating me with favoritism during those days. If only they really knew the truth that he was the only one trying to help me during my darkest night.

This resulted in higher supervision stepping in to "investigate" the matter. I was called into a meeting about my "issue." It was advised that I would need to seek counseling to deal with the trauma I had experienced so they knew that I would be fit to serve the community. I was even evaluated for a mental health hold, although there was no reason for that. As most police officers do, I denied that I needed help. My strong will and determination would be what pulled me through. I did not need counseling, especially since I could not reveal who my assailant was.

As it is with every agency, I had to attend counseling before I was allowed to return to work. Frustration set in. Fear took over. I was so afraid that others would find out about my problem, specifically the name of the officer that created the problem for me.

Fear of reprisal kept me wrapped up in dread, shame, and silence. I did not want to bring scandal to my pack. Yet I was not safe within it either.

My heart broke a little more with each passing day. My spirit wilted. I felt very betrayed at how my own team had turned their back on me. For the few people that knew of my situation, I asked for it to remain private so others would not find out. Sadly, the rumors continued to surface about me and my sergeant. None of them were true, and the worst part was that I could not stop them.

The weeks went on for me. Eventually my sergeant, the only one to listen to me, was placed on administrative leave because of an issue of sexual harassment that he was facing. I tried to fight for him because of the injustice I witnessed as a result. I could see the allegations against him taking place across the entire agency. It was never just him. It was everyone joining in.

My performance declined in the days ahead. I stopped trying my best as an officer because I was deeply struggling with the rape, and it was rapes by this point because I was powerless to stop them from happening. By now I was also struggling with the issue of my only confidant being placed on administrative leave. He was the only one to care about my problems there.

I was terrified to go to work. I began making mistakes, mostly typical rookie mistakes, because I was so afraid. I stopped seeing eye to eye with my new supervisors because I did not feel like they really cared about me. Even they shared very insensitive comments with me about the assaults.

It seemed everyone had their version of what happened to me, but nobody cared to reach out to me. My supervisors blamed me for bringing my problem to work. They even advised that I was "extremely selfish" in the matter because my problem inconvenienced them in some way. I just did not feel like they cared about me, even when I did not have to wear my sheepdog mask.

My squad mates did not communicate much with me much by this time. I found myself walking on eggshells because even they shared with supervisors their disappointment in me. Again, none of them knew of my struggles and how my one sergeant tried to help me with them. They never understood that he was not just treating me with favoritism. I struggled to go to work each day. I was afraid—afraid of my squad mates, afraid of my supervisors, afraid of my assailant. They all had power, and I was powerless. That fear overwhelmed me.

I began getting in trouble for things that happened in the squad. Even small things that would have been insignificant before everything surfaced. I was blamed for many things, even where other officers made the mistake. I took my licks and theirs and tried to press on each time. I tried to convince myself that things were going to get better, that I would do better on the next shift, even though seldom was I actually the issue. I did not deny my mistakes, but it was only that—a mistake. I never had any intent to mess up or cause problems.

I felt like this trouble was coming upon me because I made a choice to stand up for my sergeant, who did everything he could to stand up and help me in my darkest hours. I even began dealing with insensitive comments and explicit innuendos to me from my own squad mates, my own pack. In the real world, that would have been called sexual harassment, but at my agency, it was just the regular way of life. It seemed I was a target for everyone.

I reached my year of employment with the agency. My probation was extended after I hit month ten. I was told many times that I was insubordinate and did not get along well with others. I was advised that my mistakes were just too many to continue, even though many of those perceived mistakes were not mine at all.

I was told that I was argumentative and did not take criticism well from supervisors. How could I tell them that my hardest struggle was with their lack of concern and insensitive words to me during my hardest battle? How could I tell them that it was, in fact, a supervisor that had raped me? I was informed that I was no longer a good fit for the agency and that I should just resign. It seemed I had been thrown to the wolves and by my own pack, at that.

Since I was on probation, I was not truly able to stand up and fight for myself. I was walking a very thin line as it was. I requested a meeting with my command staff to speak of the injustices and my feelings. I could not say what I truly wanted to say because I was afraid of being handed a termination letter in those moments.

So once again, I had to remain silent. I took responsibility for my actions. In the end, however, it just was not enough. The next week, I was called back in and served with a termination letter. They gave me the option to resign and move on to another agency. If I chose not to resign "on my own," I would have been terminated on the spot.

My heart was broken. I had come so far and fought so hard for this dream that had just shattered before my own eyes. Who would fight for me now? Clearly it was not my agency.

At that moment, I explained to one of the commanders my true feelings. He was one of the few who knew of the rapes yet remained very unsympathetic. I told him that as much as I wanted to, I was never able to tell anyone at the agency that the rapes were done by another officer, although they already knew. I explained how I did not have the option, especially as the only female on my squad, to call out the other sheepdogs with their explicit comments and sexual treatment of me because then it would be me who paid for it with the retaliation I would face. Retaliation had already been made very real for me because of the assaults.

I advised that this problem was not just an issue with the one supervisor on leave but that it was an agency-wide issue. The commander questioned why officers did not come forward with their troubles and struggles before it erupted into a large fireball. How could we fairly come forward and fight when we would be faced with ridicule and criticism from the other sheepdogs and higher-ups? We could not be promised that we would not be targeted because of standing up for what was right. My story was proof of that.

As an officer, I still had to go to work each day and face my peers. I could not risk bringing further heartache to myself as an officer, as a person, and now a rape victim. I felt betrayed, like all my hard work and dedication meant nothing. In the end, it did not. Who will fight for me now that I am the black sheep of the blue family?

Unfortunately, this seems to be a common problem within police agencies. The media seems to portray these issues almost weekly. If we cannot get help from our own pack, our own agency, then who can we get help from? We are the only ones who truly understand what the next sheepdog is going through because we fight it every day. We are a special group of people. Most cops are truly fantastic people.

We fight so hard for those in our communities. We are not afraid to stand up for the injustices that play out before us. We sometimes forget that we need to be remembered and fought for, too, even by our own team. We are human too. At the end of our shift, we remove our mask and attempt to fit in with the rest of the world. Who will truly fight for us?

Hopefully my thoughts will bring to light the fact that we are important too. Maybe it will cause other sheepdogs to think about what one in their *own pack may be going through before they start such harsh rumors and hostile work environments. Hopefully it will show just some of the struggles that officer's experience daily, whether in the world or within the walls of our own agencies. We are worth fighting for!*

I am not sure where my journey will take me in the years to come. Perhaps the next several pages will reveal some insight on my path.

As much as I was made to feel otherwise, I am not a bad person. I was not a bad police officer. I made a difference in my short time as a sheepdog! Hopefully my tragedy will continue to make a difference in the future for others, specifically females, behind the blue line.

I will always love my job. I will always be immensely thankful for the time spent at that agency—well, up until things changed for me anyway. I learned a lot and got to meet some pretty great people along the way. Come the rise of the sun, I will boldly pick up my mask and place it back on and continue to fight the good fight. Who will fight for me? I will, because although they may be afraid of me at times, the sheep still need me, and the sheepdogs need my story more to stop this from happening again.

CHAPTER 3

Regarding the God of the universe, I often treat Him as Simon Peter did. I attempt to stand my ground and argue with Him. I speak before I think because I *think* I know what is best (Matthew 26: 31–35). I have been a King David who has broken a sacred covenant with Bathsheba, regardless of whether in the confines of marriage or merely just in my obedience to God (2 Samuel 11 and 12). I have been a Thomas who doubted the scars of Jesus (John 20:24–29). I have felt the pain of Job's wife when she told her husband to curse God and die (Job 2:11). I have been an Eve and listened to the words of Satan on more times than I wish to admit (Genesis 3). I have been a Jacob who has wrestled with God in the night (Genesis 32:22–32). I have been a Judas Iscariot who betrayed the Savior with a kiss (Luke 22). I have been a Jonah who fled from the Lord because of my own stubbornness (Jonah 1). I am a Martha because I struggle to trust in God's timing (Luke 11).

I have been arrogant and prideful. I have been broken. I have needed forgiveness repeatedly because I lack trust in the Creator of the universe because of my baggage.

How do I forgive God? My problems are not His fault. However, He seems to be the easiest to blame when something is amiss because He *could* have stopped the trouble. How do I forgive myself for allowing myself to believe in the lies of the enemy? How do I learn to love and trust again when the pain is still so real?

When I was a child, my brother murdered an innocent man. When I was twenty-four years old, my grandmother died after a long illness. Before my heart could even heal from her passing, my mother unexpectedly died three years later. A great sense of abandonment filled my soul as they both raised me into the strong and mostly confident woman that they left behind.

To date, however, one of the most difficult battles I have faced on this journey was when I was sexually assaulted by a police officer when I was twenty-nine years old. I then lost my dream job in law enforcement because I was marked as the problem. I have never been able to get back into law enforcement because somehow, I became the black sheep of the blue family.

How do I heal from this? How do I *not* blame God for not interceding on my behalf? How was He okay with stepping back while His beloved, fearfully, and wonderfully made child was experiencing such trauma and heartache? How was He able to willingly step back while Jesus was on the cross?

God, where were you? And, self, why did you put yourself in a position to allow bad things to happen to you? To your body, to your soul, to your spirit that belongs to a living and loving God?

How do you forgive God? How do you learn to be okay with yourself again after having such negative feelings about the world, about God? There are some answers that I will never have this side of heaven. Yet through it all, and despite all of the questions, God will still stand with me and strengthen me on the journey (2 Timothy 4:17).

Journal Entry

Bondage

I feel like the world hates me, like they only view me as just another sexual deviant who apparently sleeps around with everything that moves. Oh, and then slaps my "prey" with a rape allegation. I feel like the surrounding world lacks trust in me because I finally found the courage to break free from the bondage of silence and talk about the sexual assaults that have haunted me and held me captive for months. The physical pain of each rape is over now, but the emotional pain and scars left behind runs deep.

I feel like those watching me degradingly tell me that I am just another liar looking for attention, that I am just out to ruin someone's life. I feel like they constantly talk poorly of me because I must have done something to bring this upon myself. They will be nice to my face, but they secretly hate every fiber of my being because there is no way someone of such a high caliber could commit a rape against someone like—well, me.

What they do not realize is that I had never slept with anyone before I was raped. They refuse to believe that I was a virgin before this assault. What they do not care to see is that my heart is pure and innocent, and alleging something like a rape is a very serious matter which I would not just make up. My high morals and faith in God would not allow that.

I am not out to ruin someone's life. I never was. I never wanted this, but I feel blamed by everyone and especially by the police department. Mostly, I feel like I cannot be loved because I do not deserve it since I spoke up.

Am I not worth it? Can I never be loved because of these unfortunate circumstances? Will I ever be given a chance to redeem myself, even though I have never lied about any of this? It feels like I will never be given a *proper chance to fairly get past this because surely, I did something wrong in the matter. It is like people are afraid of me, afraid of what I could do or say about my next "victim." What nobody understands is that I am, in fact, the true victim, having to relive this nightmare repeatedly with each rising sun. I was the one who was raped, not my assailant.*

It hurts. Not only physically during the rapes but emotionally after the rapes. Not just from my assailant but from those around me who do not understand my struggle, who do not understand how it feels to be living through this nightmare. Who cowardly judge me because they are unaware and uneducated on the true problem. Who share callous words with me that do cut into my already wounded heart and mind.

When does it end for me? When do I get justice? When can I really be loved again? When do I get the opportunity to fairly make it within the police world again? Can I? Will I? Will I ever be given that chance? I wonder if there will ever be a day when someone will look past my scars and see something, well, beautiful and worth taking a chance on. I wonder if the day will ever come when others will not be afraid to even look at me for fear of being sent straight to the very pits of hell.

For now, though, my heart cries.

How long will the world hold me in their bondage? It is bad enough my memories of those moments hold me there as it is. I just long to feel normal again, but normalcy is something I will never know. How long until I truly get to be free again? Am I even worth it anyway?

Journal Entry

Utter Confusion

All of me is filled with utter confusion. Torn emotions in which I am clueless to face. Do I laugh? Do I cry? Do I get angry or even run away? Do I boast a banner of strength even though that facade is sure to come crashing down like an avalanche of loose rocks? Why does my mind believe the lies and false beliefs from past experiences?

My mind tells me that I am not beautiful. It tells me I am a fake. My emotions tell me I am unworthy. They tell me I do not deserve to be loved. My spirit tells me I am fractured and that the pieces cannot be fixed. My body tells me it longs to experience a true love and not something like the hurt and pain the past has brought me.

I live in utter confusion, true bafflement because I want to be beautiful, worthy, and glued together in one piece. Yet how can that ever happen after this harsh experience haunts me? How do I get past the pain? How do I see life as something beautiful again? How do I even see me as someone beautiful who is fearfully and wonderfully made?

My recent past is dark, very dark. Not by my own volition but by the hands of a manipulator who knew how to steal and destroy his prey. The hurts come daily because through his masterful tactics, I am the one who feels like a failure. It is me who feels inhibited because I completely missed all the signs of the danger lurking ahead. How was I so blind to his ways? How do I forgive myself for missing the signs? Maybe because I missed the Danger Ahead signs, I deserved what happened? How does anyone deserve that? Because of him, I may never feel beautiful, worthy, or put together again.

I guess I will just hide deeper within myself in a feeble attempt to protect myself in the hope that maybe, just maybe, one day, I can be put back together again. Until then, the shards of each piece of me will continue to cut deep. This wound is left open and exposed; it is a daily and painful existence that I live because one person hurt me.

The Bible says that joy comes in the morning. I am asking, when does morning come?

Journal Entry

The Exam

The room was cold and lonely even though there were four other women in there with me. It was stale with an eerie stench that seemed more than I could handle. I felt numb to my surroundings even though they screamed of my situation. How could I be in here? How could this be my story now?

My thoughts were immediately interrupted by a "Ma'am, I need you to remove each article of clothing and place them in this bag." One by one, each article of clothing was carefully removed and handed off to the nurse. I had nothing left.

I was then asked to lie down on the hard, narrow, and cold surface to begin the process with nothing more than an open hospital gown on my stiff and injured body. I solemnly lay there, openly exposed to a perfect stranger, while they carefully performed each step of the exam.

I cautiously listened to each instruction, trying my best to focus just enough to answer each question as I could remember from the events of the day. My body was slowly and methodically searched, inside and out. I felt violated for the second time that day.

The bright lights, coupled with the lingering thoughts of the day, had caused a headache of the century. Immense shame and guilt filled every inch of my being as these women, whom I did not know, intricately searched for marks, bruises, and foreign matter. I wanted to hide, but all I could do was hide my face deep into a pillow that had been given to me during the process.

Naked. Afraid. Alone and being stared at by complete strangers. I lay there fighting back harsh tears and bitter anger. For this was a rape exam, and I was the victim.

Journal Entry

Help Is on the Way

I am not a counselor or a therapist of any kind. In fact, I am sure that I give my therapist a run for his money every time I go see him. I am almost positive that after some sessions, he would rather just hang me up by my toenails—from the ceiling rafters. Then I am sure he makes a beeline to see his own therapist because foolish people do exist in this world. Instead, he simply responds with compassion and empathy to help me sort through my messy emotions.

In the days following the assaults, I struggled to admit that I needed help from anyone. My strong will, sometimes-haughty independence, and high amount of shame kept me in silence. Besides, I was a fully grown adult! I should not have needed help because adults are supposed to have all the answers, or so I thought.

The truth is, I did struggle, greatly! I struggled with who I was as a person. I did not want to believe that something this heinous could happen to me, a cop, at that. I did not want to admit that someone I trusted could take something so personal from me. I just could not admit that I was raped. I knew it was true, but isn't "admitting" the hardest step for anyone with a problem?

It took me awhile to tell anyone of the crime that had been committed. When I did, I hid like a puppy who had just chewed up his master's shoes as I spoke about it. I did not want anyone to see my brokenness. I did not want them to see that I was, in fact, the foolish one because this happened to me. I felt immense shame. Talking about it was my first real hurdle because that meant that it was actually real and that I could encounter trouble for reporting it.

I remember telling a close family friend several days after the first occurrence. I really did not know what to do, and he seemed to be the best and safest option for me since he generally allowed me to speak freely with him. He sat patiently and listened to my anger, my tears, my pain. He watched me hide behind a couch pillow as I shared the details. He did not judge me but allowed me to feel as much comfort as I was able to receive, given the lack of trust I now had for men.

A few weeks later, after an assault happened a second time, I informed my sergeant at the police department that I had been taken advantage of in my personal life. Even with being given very few details about the event, he was ready to go to battle for me. I am almost sure I saw steam coming from his ears and fire being breathed from his mouth as he thought of how he could handle this issue. He, too, did not judge me but explained to me that I was not at fault, and most importantly, that I was not alone!

I began to withdraw deep within myself, both in my personal life and in my professional life. I would stay in bed for hours on end when I was at home, and I would go sit alone and hide under the trees at the local park when I was at work. I did not continue to speak of the assaults as I was not safe. I needed help, and I knew it, but I was trying to salvage even the slightest bit of dignity I had left.

As the days and months—many months—went on, I slowly started opening up about my skeletons in the closet. My best friend cried and yelled when I told her. My brother was ready to get on a plane home to handle the situation when he was informed. My place of employment targeted me and then forced me to resign when I told them. Others, still, had the audacity to judge and blame me for the assaults because surely, I did something to bring this about. I lost friends as a result. I guess tragedy and hardships really do show you who your real friends are after all. However, then there were some friends that drew ever close to me to show that they truly cared even through my great amount of resistance.

I kept it fairly quiet, but the more I spoke of the assaults to my friends, the more I learned that several of them had also been assaulted at some point in their lives. I had known these friends for years and never knew that about them, because so many rape victims suffer in silence to save themselves from more heartache and additional trauma. It really is easier to stay quiet than to try to talk about a topic most of the world knows nothing about. The terrible statistic is that one in six women and one in thirty-three men will be raped in their lifetime. Most victims remain silent about their experience. The numbers are staggering! I knew nothing about this, until it happened to me.

By proxy, my friends were now involved, whether they wanted to be or not. Yes, I felt terrible about that because this was not something they needed to shoulder. Some advised they did not want to be dragged into this issue and then quickly fled from my life but only after they prodded for details. Others, however, stood steadfastly by and made sure I got out of bed or even just ate a meal since that, too, was a huge struggle for me. Some would sit with me the entire night long as I contemplated life in my severe depression. They refused to give up on me because they saw my true worth as a person. Despite my circumstances, they saw my beauty. They knew I was not foolish or to blame. They were trying to restore my dignity as a female.

I still struggle to get help with things. It is just not in my nature to be out of control of a situation. When I am not in control, it sends me into a silent tailspin until I can figure out how to get things back on track again. I like my world packed neatly into a box and not spilled out for everyone to see. I like control, which is something that was taken from me when I was assaulted. The fact of the matter is, we all need help at different times in our lives. We were not created to handle life alone. Even the Bible speaks of "where two or three are gathered." We were not created for isolation but association with others, even when the storms of life roll in.

Whether you struggle with a rape or a financial problem, a sick family member, or a lack of self-worth, or maybe something as simple as a bad grade on a test, seek out help. You will be awestruck at how many people will come to your rescue with their kindness when you truly need it. Maybe it is a meal or gas money or simply just needing to get out of bed each day, someone will be there to help. Pride will keep you in silence. Trust the counselor, the friend, the coworker. Talk to someone, but do not face the struggles alone. Get the help you need so you can enjoy life again.

As with any trauma, it will get messy. You will be fearful and exhausted. You may cry. You may even gain an eating disorder, a drug habit, or even contemplate suicide. I promise, though, that help is on the way if you just ask for it!

CHAPTER 4

One thing I still force myself to believe is that God *is* good and that He has a great purpose for the pain. He does not waste trauma. He equips the called. He sends His people into the uttermost parts of the world to proclaim His promise of love and salvation because He *is* love despite all the hate in the world.

Trauma, tragedy, pain, turmoil, etc. is made to hurt because the enemy is good at his job. He is the father of lies and deceit. There is *no* truth in him (John 8:44). So why do we allow him to have so much power and access to our heart, soul, emotions, and mind? Why then, when bad things happen, do we not just immediately blame him instead of God?

For those in Christ, the answer is tragically simple. When things go wrong, we tend to blame those closest to us. The person who is closest to us, or who should be at least, and who knows us the best *is* God if He lives in our hearts. He knows our down sittings and our uprisings (Psalm 139:2). He is attentive to our going out and our coming in (Psalm 121:8). He is fully aware that His power is made perfect in our weaknesses (2 Corinthians 12:9). Yet we still treat Him with utter despair when life gets hard.

When Lazarus died, Jesus wept (John 11:35). It has been said that He wept because Lazarus was His friend. Another perspective of why He wept was because of the people's unbelief in Him. Jesus weeps for us. He weeps for us in our pain and hurts. Probably like any good father, He desires to take away our heartaches. He also weeps because we stop trusting in His power in our lives when the storms roll in.

The truth is that God allows us to go through storms in life just to show us that He *can* still calm the winds and the waves (Mark 4:29). Whether it is to the storm itself as it rumbles or to our weary soul as it trembles, He still comes along and gently whispers, "Peace be still," and the storms bow down again.

God will calm a storm or move a mountain if we choose to believe and have the faith of a mustard seed in Him that it *can* be done (Matthew 17:20–21). Sometimes, the only thing you have left in life is an *ounce* of faith. Yet an ounce, a mustard seed, is all you really need.

I had a professor in college, who has since gone home to be with the Lord, share an insightful perspective to his students regarding mountaintops and valleys. He stated that mountaintops are just for perspective. Things do not grow on the mountaintop, but they do grow in the valley. Next time you see a mountain, take a look at where the tree line ends; it is not usually at the top.

What valley are you in today? How can you grow through it? Or are you standing tall on the mountaintop learning just how much God kept you in the palm of His hands as you climbed to that point? The interesting point to remember is this: the God on the mountain *is* still the same God in the valley (Psalm 23).

Journal Entry

No Exemptions!

I am a law enforcement officer. I arrest people for a living. I drive hastily to hot calls to save others. I love my job because I love my community, and I only want what is best for them!

I was a law enforcement officer, anyway.

Within my job, I saw evil in each shift I worked. I did not have the ability to live a "normal" life because I chose this career, and I would not trade it for anything in the world either. I always watch the hands of others. I always look for bulges of weapons and watch body language, etc. because that is the way I have been trained. Trust nobody because evil is lurking! It is merely a matter of time before it rears its ugly head.

Evil, just like sin, can be wrapped up in a cute little package just waiting to attack. A little old lady can be just as dangerous as the drug dealer with a gun. I have seen it.

Evil can also be wrapped up in a police uniform carrying a gun and a badge. Nobody is exempt. Unfortunately, nobody is exempt from being the victim of such horrific crimes either. Negatively but honestly speaking, it is all just a matter of time. Why make it easier for people to prey on others? Seems like victims do not really matter anymore because nothing is being done for them. They deserve justice too!

More importantly, before they even have a chance at becoming the next victim, they deserve to be made aware that such evil does exist. Maybe it will save them some heartache along their journey, because there are no exemptions on who could be affected!

I, myself, have experienced it. The heartache, the shame, the painful recourse of someone's actions. Not only was I a police officer, but I was also the victim of a sexual battery (rape). Some days, I cannot even leave my house because I am so afraid of what may happen when I leave the confines of my home, the home that I was supposed to be safe in. After experiencing that, I cannot help but constantly think of what the motives of others could be. I live in a constant state of fear not knowing what someone is thinking or planning.

In my situation, I never saw it coming. I knew the person that assaulted me. Approximately 82 percent of sexual assault survivors do know who hurt them. He assaulted me more than once because I was too afraid to speak up about it. I was terrified that nobody would believe me because, in the end, they did not. I was minimized. I fight each day wondering when it could happen again because he still lives in my community.

Why is that? Why do the people that matter rarely believe the victims of sexual assault? I understand that it is not what you know, but it is what you can prove. Even with very little or no proof, I am still a victim, and now a survivor, because the crime happened to me. I guess that is another frustrating thought for another day, however.

Remember that only twenty-five out of every one thousand rapists will spend time in jail. That leaves the rest of them to walk free.

Some may say, "Well, you are the police officer. You are the very definition of protection and service. You should be able to protect yourself." In my own trying times, I could not. Now have no doubt in my abilities as an officer. It was always such an easy task to care for those I swore to protect and serve. I was rarely afraid when I wore my uniform. I would jump in feetfirst and seek out the trouble hiding in the bushes. I did well to protect others and myself when I put on my uniform. Yet in my own time, I could not protect myself because I was weak. I was afraid. I was silenced.

It seems almost like an oxymoron, to be a police officer and a weak and powerless victim.

I cannot tell you exactly why I was raped. I did not even see it coming. I did not know evil was on the horizon because there were no warning signs. The question of why it happened still lingers in my mind, begging to be answered. The answer is something that I will never have, nor will I get an apology. I can say that it took all control away from me during those moments. I felt helpless as I lay there because I was unable to fight against his power. My pleas to stop were ignored. The pain I spoke of went unheard. Yet I was still a cop.

The truth of the matter is that my position and stature within the community has nothing to do with being a victim of a crime. There are no exemptions! I could have been a doctor, a lawyer, a teacher, a college student, a librarian, a transient, a Walmart cashier, or a twelve-year-old child because unfortunately, none of us are exempt from the evils of others. My assailant knew I was a police officer, and he was one too.

Do I wish I could go back and change everything? Absolutely! Do I wish I could have been smarter and saw the signs ahead of the crime? I sure do! Unfortunately, I cannot change anything now. Even as a police officer, this is now a part of my journey, my story.

I cannot change it; so while I can, I will make others aware of the evil that is lurking to save them from possibly being hurt too. It is shameful and scary. I would not wish this to happen to anyone.

I am no longer a police officer. Not only did my assailant take away my control, my freedom, my power, even my virginity, he also took away my job as well, my dream, all because of his selfish actions.

There are no exemptions! Be vigilant! Be cognizant! Be always aware of your surroundings! Do not be the next victim because it truly can happen to anyone!

Journal Entry

I Had a Plan!

I feel like such a failure in life! I have worked so hard and come so far—for nothing. I have always wanted my life to be different. I had a plan that would never allow for mediocrity, that would never accept handouts, that would never put me in a place of complete helplessness in which I would have to rely on others. I had a goal to accomplish greatness and to be the very best at what I tried my hand at. Although I am not perfect whatsoever, I had a plan!

My plan was beautiful. It was meticulously patterned out to where even the smallest details were taken care of. I would not disappoint anyone, especially myself. I would get the best job and bring laughter and joy to those around me with my unpredictable antics. I would support myself, pay my bills, and save for some greater purpose. I had a plan!

My plan was coming to fruition nicely as I had a great job, a nice place to live, and a handful of true friends by my side. According to those around me, my personality was the life of every party. Life was fun! I felt humbly accomplished. I was the happiest I had been in years because my dreams were made into my reality. I loved my job! Essentially, I loved my life. I was doing well for myself.

Suddenly and without warning, my plan shattered into a million tiny pieces. I fell into a tumultuous storm that raged about like a category 4 hurricane. My "lights" were out. My dreams, broken. My life was a mess within just a matter of a few minutes. My storm had taken my passion, my job, my self-worth, my dignity, even my virginity. My neatly packaged world could now be declared as a disaster zone.

I wandered in this disaster zone in disbelief and shock. I felt like I had lost everything true about me. I lost my identity. I lost my independence. I lost my freedom. I lost my joy of life. Now all I found myself doing was staying in bed all day, rarely eating a meal, and shutting down from everything. I hated myself because of my circumstances. I felt like a failure because surely, I had messed up somewhere along the way.

My plan had been ruined. I was now in a place of mediocrity, handouts, and reliance on others because I could not take care of myself, physically and emotionally. I could not even keep myself safe, and this storm was proof of that.

I still face the aftereffects of the rolling winds of the storm. Instead of a declaration of a disaster zone, I should probably just be declared condemned. I am without a law enforcement job, with rejections on each new application I submit. My quaint little apartment is no longer a safe haven, as I cannot live there or even live alone right now. My nights have become completely restless and riddled with violent nightmares of my trial. Some friends have disappeared into the night, so my mess cannot spill over into their perfect plans. Going out in public has become very limited for me because fear keeps me indoors. Even my faith has become fragile with utter despair.

But God.

Through it all, I can see God's hand sustaining me. Barely. Although the tears have nearly blinded my eyes. In my spirit, I know that He is holding me when I am ready to completely give up on the journey. He has provided for my needs, be it financial or in just eating a meal. He has given me safe places to lay my head each night since the storm started. He has given me friends who are willing to stand by my side and listen—listen to me vent, listen to me cry, listen to me try to cope with my situation. He has sent the right people along the way to shield me from the strong winds and heavy rains. They have helped me shelter in place.

My initial plan was ruined. It did not turn out how I had expected it should or would. Yet God has picked up the pieces of my life and has held them ever close to His heart. He has shown me that He loves me in a thousand different ways. Although I am cracked now, it is those cracks that His light will shine through, for me and for others.

Please, God, calm the storm, but if you choose to keep me here for a bit longer, then please give me peace and rest in the storm.

I had a plan for my life. It was a plan that ultimately weakened my faith, my might, my willpower, and me. It turns out that it was my plan and not God's plan for me. Yet God has shown me repeatedly that His plans are greater than mine and that it is in Him that I will be made strong because He is my rock and fortress. I question now why I am going through this storm because I despise it! However, I am confident that I will look back some time from now and see that what Satan meant for evil, God used for my good and, ultimately, for His glory!

Journal Entry

Apartment 108

I closed the door to apartment 108 for the last time today. I wish this was some symbolic display from life that meant I was also closing that chapter as well. Regrettably, though, that chapter is still writing itself even though the lock to a past heartache was securely latched for the final time.

I do not remember looking in the rearview mirror as I drove away from my apartment. I was trying not to look back to the dreary past of the last ten months in which I lived there. For seldom do I remember joyful laughter filling each room of the house; rather, I could see the dreadful pain that resonated inside me each time I walked in the door.

Now do not get me wrong. There were some good days, like the Christmas party. We laughed until our souls were joyful, and we ate until the crowd had to be rolled home. I also remember watching the cat frolic around from time to time, placing smiles on the faces of all who watched him. Yet the good days were very few and far between.

I loved my little apartment. When I first moved into the home, it felt as if I had done something right to live there. It was my place. Along with it being my own place came a true sense of freedom every twenty-something-year-old desires to have: no rules; no bedtime; no curfew; oh, and ice cream for breakfast, lunch, and dinner was an accepted and welcomed item on the menu. I loved life. The life in which I was proud of. I enjoyed calling apartment 108 home.

As time went on, my home eventually became more of a prison for me. The very place in which I was supposed to be safe was the very place that I was wounded at my deepest. I no longer enjoyed going home. When I did, I hid *in my room, away from anyone else who stopped in for a visit. I was no longer safe in my home. The memories plagued me as I stayed there.*

If the walls could tell a story, they would reveal the deep dark secrets of what went on inside of them. They would scream of the many rapes that occurred while I lived there. They would reveal just how many pleadings to stop went ignored. They would tell of the dreadful pain each rape brought about. So would the police department walls, for that matter.

The walls would share of my severe weight loss and deep depression as a result. They would probably yell out how I hurt my own body because of the wounded and broken spirit I carried around. They would speak of the many tears I cried after the painful moments were over. They would explain to anyone willing to listen of the utter confusion that overtook me and my soul during those days. They would recount the very difficult moments of allowing the police to come in to investigate the crime of sexual battery, not caring much about my dignity. If the walls could talk, they would share so many deep dark secrets in which I care to never remember or relive.

It was a bittersweet day today. In between packing the moving truck and throwing last-minute items into boxes, I fought back tears and raw emotions that filled my heart. I said goodbye to what felt like my freedom and independence, even though that was taken away long ago by my assailant. I even yelled at God a little bit for completely flipping my perfect little life inside out!

As I left, I whispered a word of hope for the next tenants who would reside there. I then waved goodbye to the harsh memories that replayed daily as I entered my room. The very memories that was once my reality. I stood at the entrance to what was my room and held hope that the sleepless nights and violent nightmares would stay there and not follow me to my next place.

I said goodbye to the city that betrayed me. I waved so long to the police department that made me fight alone against their police officer for months. I also said goodbye to all my trust for the local law enforcement since they showed me their true colors in my case.

My heart breaks a little bit because all of this is just a constant reminder of how I feel that I have failed in and at life. As I look back now, maybe apartment 108 was the tool in which God will make His glory known through me and maybe make me a little bit stronger along the way.

I wish I could change everything about those ten months. I would love to go back to the early weeks of joyful glee I had and somehow carve out a new path there. However, I cannot. I will not know the purpose of the pain for a while still—if I ever even find out. Even as much as I kicked and screamed at times, I am thankful that God held me close to His heart during that dark journey.

I am safe now. I can lay my head on my pillow in peace knowing that my body will not be hurt again! I am sure the nightmares will be ever present as this chapter is not closed yet. At least I can now work on getting past the feelings of inadequacy, failure, and intense hurt I carry deep within my soul. I can slowly start to safely carve out a new life beyond apartment 108.

Now where are my Rollerblades? I have a new neighborhood to go explore.

Journal Entry

Sleepless Sheep

One sheep. Two sheep. Three sheep. Four.

Well, it is yet another sleepless night, but I guess I would rather have sleepless than a night riddled with violent nightmares. It seems there is no equal balance, however. I just wish life would go back to normal. So while I recount sleepless sheep with my utterly confused mind, let me recount my day and the feelings that accompanied it.

I paid a visit to my doctor today, a very long and overdue visit to him. I did my best to avoid the situation, but I could not do so any longer. I took a close friend with me as they could speak the words I needed to say yet could not muster up. Just as my fears would reveal, my doctor prescribed me an antidepressant medication.

I am not crazy, or maybe I am. That has yet to be determined, in my mind at least. Apparently, my closest friends tell a different story. That is usually just in fun, though.

I have always viewed depression medication as a weakness. My mother took it all of my life, and she was the strongest person I knew, out in public. She masked it well, but I always saw her in the darkest of midnight as weak as a newborn kitten runt struggling to stay alive. I never wanted to be depressed and forced to take medications because I saw what it did to her. However, just as she had to, I find myself in need of them as well during this season of life because of the sexual trauma. Hopefully through my deepest weakness and greatest trauma, I will grow ever strong and beat this in time.

I sat around a campfire tonight pouring my heart out to a bunch of people who really do not understand my journey. Yes, some of them have experienced *sexual assault and probably worse than mine. I still felt alone and empty as I shared my story. I still feel at fault because of masterful manipulation tactics, although I know I am not to blame and never was. I feel like there is a purpose for this pain, but I have not found it yet.*

My story probably did not change lives tonight. It did not make much of a difference to anyone that listened. It just served as a painful reminder that just as the campfire we gazed upon, my life is in the raging fire too. Unfortunately, the difference is that my fire is not peaceful and relaxing. It does not have the ability to roast delicious marshmallows over it while belting out a crazy rendition of Kumbaya. It only can char my soul to a mere pile of ash. It has placed a stronghold on my mind, which causes this depression I now face.

My emotions could not be more confused right now! I am angry and want to run away and hide, but I want my story to make a difference too. My life is ashes, but I need to fan the embers and fight on to victory.

Where is my journey taking me? What is the purpose for this experience? Will it change lives? Will it create some spectacular movement within law enforcement? Will it make a change that I so desperately want to see within the police department? I am not sure, so until I know, I must figure out how to keep myself strong enough to fan the embers another day. I must discover how to get past the nightmares and sleeplessness. I must learn how to smile and laugh once again. I guess I must figure out how to be "content in whatsoever state I am in" (Philippians 4:11), even if the fire is raging. Even when my sleepless sheep head count has reached a million.

Until then, perhaps liquid melatonin, coupled with my new depression medication, is the answer. Well, at least I will be helping their causes stay alive for now.

Five sheep. Six sheep. Seven sheep. A million. Good night, world.

Journal Entry

Chapters

I feel like God has done just what most of my friends have done in my life. He has quietly exited stage left of this chapter of my life. If He has, I cannot blame Him, because who in their right mind wants to be part of this? Of me? I push people away. Yes, unfortunately, even God too.

I am in this stage of grief where I have never felt so alone and abandoned before. I feel rage building up in my soul because of how unlovable I am. I feel as if I have lost control of my mind. I hate that! I feel like nobody is standing in my corner anymore. I cannot blame them either.

I just long to feel normal again, but I do not. I want so desperately to be loved. I want to know that someone wants to care for and fight with me. I want to trust, but I just cannot. I seldom wonder if I ever will.

I often wonder if this life is even worth it anymore. I keep trying to hold out to see what the next chapter writes. For this one is dark and dreary, and I am ready to finish. I am ready to leave this chapter unfinished because I just cannot deal with the pain etched into the pages anymore. I know I have a lot of life ahead of me. Ironically, I still hold the hope that God will do something amazing with my story, but the words on my pages are beginning to run from all the tears I have cried. They are becoming unreadable. My pages have become crinkled from trying to erase and hide all the mistakes. My binding is slowly falling apart. Just like my life has for years now. Will my story be finished? Will it have a happy ending? Will someone else find healing and hope within my pages? Will I find healing and hope in a chapter soon?

I am running out of tears to cry. My faith is dwindling. My purpose is unclear. I am just not sure how much longer I can hold on. Especially with how alone and abandoned I feel by everyone. I just wish I could be normal again. For now, however, I will put my pen down and close the pages for the night. Maybe tomorrow, my new chapter will begin. Hopefully anyway, because I truly do not know how much more this battered and weary soul can handle in this chapter.

Journal Entry

Broken

My mind, body, and soul are broken! I am at the place where I just cannot fix them anymore, nor do I wish to even try. Just when I feel like I have taken two steps forward with progress, failure, heartbreak, and emotions whisk me four giant steps back. I feel like a prisoner trapped in my own body. What is worse is that I do not know how to convey my feelings to anyone else to make them understand what the aftermath of sexual assault feels like.

Like the good little patient that I am, I go to therapy almost every week. I really enjoy seeing my therapist, as I feel safe there. The therapist has been a true blessing to me over the months. I am almost positive that person is just an angel wrapped in human flesh.

I have come a long way since I first started therapy. I cannot go to the office without crying through each session. (Yes, this "tough" former cop does cry.) I still hide my body with the couch pillows, and I fail miserably at maintaining eye contact, but I have progressed. A lot!

Until this week.

Part of my story, and the reason why I go to therapy, has recently hit the news. My name was not shared, but the story was featured on almost every channel across the area. My heart broke as I watched each segment. Now that was probably the worst thing for me to do, but I just had to know what they were saying and how I was being conveyed. Contrary to all popular belief, I do care greatly about what people think about me.

I found myself feeling defeated and moping around because I cannot control my emotions after the articles were published. My heart hurts. It is angry. My spirit is broken. I feel like I have been forsaken. I am lost. Yet their lies of what happened to me seems to prevail.

I cannot make it through the night anymore without having a violent nightmare of these encounters. When I can sleep, it is incredibly restless, as I cannot get certain images out of my mind. The face of my assailant is constantly flashing through my mind. So any healing that has taken place with my therapist has just been destroyed by the media. My fears. My nightmares. My emotions.

My latest nightmare was that my assailant found me, and when he did, he hurled angry rage at me for ruining his life. He then handed me his service pistol and yelled at me to finish the job. He screamed for me to kill him—with his own gun. Once again, he ignored my plea of "No!" as he raged on.

That nightmare was incredibly vivid and violent. I was shattered and shaking, not just during the dream but after I was able to awaken myself from it. Then just as always, the nightmares continued, once again, after I was finally able to fall back asleep again.

Going to sleep scares me just about as much as staying awake does. I just cannot win.

Will I ever heal? Will the journey ever smooth out and be okay again? Will my spirit be restored? Will my mind be free of the pain it has known for so long? Will my heart be reconciled? Will I ever feel loved and worthy again?

Even for more simple things in life, will I ever be able to comfortably leave my home again without constantly watching over my shoulder? Will I ever be able to sleep again? Will the nightmares ever stop? When does true healing come?

I have lost my fight and nearly the last ounce of faith I have left in me. I feel that I am at the place where I just cannot fix the brokenness anymore, nor do I wish to even try.

Journal Entry

Victim of a Rape

I'm afraid to go in public now,
I stay and hide within,
I plan my days out carefully
In fear of seeing him.
I still don't know what I did wrong
Although I've cast my claim,
I feel as if I'm at fault,
Does he feel the same?
He made me feel that I'm to blame
Within his callous jest,
I could only lay in silent pain
With opposition to his quest.
Does he see that he did wrong?
Even in my deepest plea,
When my words went ignored,
As he took a piece of me.
Does he know the pain he caused
Has scarred me deep within,
And will stay with me forever now,
In this "new" life that I live.
I have lost my smile now,
And all good things of me,
I no longer share in laughter deep,
That once rang wild and free.

I cry myself to sleep now,
As my days are dark and dim,
As images flash through my mind
Of that painful time with him.
My nights are filled with nightmares,
That overtake my sleep,
And the loneliness I feel inside
Just causes me to weep.
Fear has taken over me,
I'm anxious at my best,
All because one selfish soul
Has brought me in this mess.
I carry around a title now,
I'm a statistic with no name,
A life that was once beautiful,
Now deeply filled with shame.
And worse yet now I sit and wait
For justice that I crave,
For this senseless tragedy
That will hold me till my grave.
I try to make some sense of this,
The questions fill my mind,
And now I rest in the fact
That answers I won't find.
Life is not so simple now,
My fear has me restrained,
Will the peace I used to know

Ever break me from these chains?
Or will I stay bound up tight,
With nary an escape,
Where the only name I'll ever know is
"Victim of a rape."

But I've stood up to the system now,
A hero with no shame,
No longer can he hold me as
A victim of his game.
Because strength will be my banner now
I've overcome great odds,
And even when I've questioned most,
I'm still so loved by God.
I will always have the memories,
But those moments are at rest,
I can lay my head in solitude
And know I did my best.
The questions that remain in me,
Are settled with resolve,
And will push me on to greater heights,
Although they stay unsolved.
I have conquered on this journey now,
To help those in my stead,
To have a brighter sojourn here
On the path that lies ahead.
And if now if what I've been through

Can help one on their way,
The evil that was done to me,
Was a blessing in delay.
I don't wish this on an enemy,
But I won't live as before,
My assailant has no hold on me,
For now, and evermore.
No longer am I silenced now,
In the evil brought by one,
I will speak of onward victory
Until my race is run.
He no longer has his grasp on me,
I have found my great escape,
Where never will I live again
As a "victim of a rape."

CHAPTER 5

Much of my disbelief and frustration at God came because of my sexual assaults. I was incredibly innocent and naive prior to that time in my life. Then like a thief in the night, Satan struck. Just when I thought I was comfortable in life, in my dream career, he sent a proverbial tornado to stir up trouble. Without warning and without any preparation for the destruction it was going to leave behind. It was an EF5 tornado.

I was caught off guard. I did not really know that there could be such destruction in the world, especially when the destruction was wearing a police uniform. Yes, I knew about my brother's crimes when I was a child. It was heartbreaking for my family. I had many mixed-up emotions when I was advised that he took an innocent life after he had already spent years destroying ours. However, that was all toward someone else, not *really* me. Besides all the confusion from that, I really did not have a reason to distrust God, until something happened *to me*.

Once trust is broken, it is very hard to get it back. So as anyone can imagine, it has taken years for me to be fully okay with God again. Remember, we take our greatest fears, anger, and distrust out on those who are the closest to us. Sometimes my heart breaks for God because of the way *I* treat Him in my own pain. I forget that He also experienced a great pain when His Son died on the cross to save the world.

I am not there yet. However, I maintain the hope that God will use my story for His purpose, because I refuse to believe that He wastes anything, including pain. If I am willing, He can and will use me to point others to Him and hopefully to help others learn how to heal from their own baggage.

Now, that will take time, because after someone breaks into your body, it is very difficult to move past that. Rape is a crime that does not just happen *during* the act. It repeatedly manifests and unfolds in its aftermath, too, in the way of nightmares, new fears, hatred, mistrust, confusion, etc. Silence tends to befall the victims (survivors) because the shame of the act is just too heavy to bear. So we tend to carry it alone, fight it alone, because our voice has been silenced, including by those within the justice system at times.

Did Jesus weep for me? Did He weep for the lost soul of the man who did that to my body? Did He cry when He took my mother home to be with Him in heaven? Did He mourn when He saw His child mourning the loss of their loved one?

> Blessed are those who mourn, for they shall be comforted. (Matthew 5:4 ESV)

I did not feel comforted when the pain was the most evident. Does He still feel the nails when I sin? What about when I sin willfully? Does Jesus hurt because of me? Because of my baggage?

I have always heard the analogy to leave your burdens and baggage at the foot of the cross. How do you do that? Your baggage is not necessarily an actual object that can just be laid down and left somewhere. Yes, the pain of the physical trauma is over, but the emotions and scars left behind are not physical items that can just be thrown away like a piece of trash. Without an actual animate object to let go of, it is difficult to fully understand how to rid our deepest being of our most tragic hurts. It is even harder to *trust* God with them.

It is hard to keep the faith in anything after something wounds us to our core. Perhaps the crater-sized wound is that our marriage broke up or our child died. Maybe there is a spouse who struggles with viewing inappropriate images, or we were just diagnosed with a major illness. Perhaps we were raped. It all hurts, and it hurts people differently. It can be very difficult to keep the faith in times of trouble.

I know that God is real, but I often question if He is real in *my* life. Sometimes, I cannot help but ask the same questions I have asked multiple times over the past few years: *God, where are you? Why do you feel so far away from me? I just need you to make yourself known to me because you have not felt real in so long.*

His answer? A gentle stir then washes over my mind and heart as only God could. To my dismay, a still small voice immediately reminds me that anger, bitterness, guilt, and shame have taken up so much space in my heart that there was never any room for Him to come in. I feel remorseful knowing that I have probably grieved Him and left Him out for so long that I was never able to hear Him because of my deep hurt.

It is important to remember that our past was a lesson, not a life sentence. By choosing to remain in anger, bitterness, guilt, and shame, it is simply us choosing a life sentence over freedom in Christ. The battle belongs to the Lord, and He will fight for you if you hand Him the key to the prison cell you have built for yourself.

We would all like to say that we will be strong during our trials. We believe that we will remain confident in our abilities and skills when the waves are crashing to and fro. We hope that we will respond a certain way if an EF5 tornado does strike in our lives. However, we are then let down within ourselves, and with God, when something different happens. We do not know how to handle it when our mental expectations are different from our physical reality. We do not know how to cope when all the training we have received throughout life is nowhere to be found when we are faced with a traumatic situation. Tunnel vision is real, whether in our physical being or in our emotional brokenness.

For example, I never thought I would be a victim of rape or be left by my mother when she died. I thought I could handle it if something bad came my way, because my mother raised a very strong-willed and independent girl. I was sorely disappointed in myself when my reactions to my trauma and tragedy were different than how I expected it should be. It was also mind-altering when I saw how others handled the same scenarios differently and seemingly better than I was able to, which further escalated the feelings of shame and defeat. Where was the strength within me in the face of the battle?

I was also confused within my heart when others shared how I *should* have reacted instead, even from those who had never been through the same trauma. I should have been stronger. I should not have been afraid to speak up. I should not have been as affected as I was because I thought I could handle life when it got tough. Even those around me shared that same message. So naturally, I became frustrated within myself and with God when my life took a downward spiral.

Troubles and trials will come. That is, unfortunately, a reality because of the world that we live in. The good news is that God has overcome the world (John 16:33). Just as He did when He walked this earth, we will all experience some form of trouble or trial along the journey. It will not always be pretty. It may not even be manageable. We may feel defeated. Getting out of bed or eating a meal may even become a challenge when we do. Knowing who you can love and trust will get murky when you are walking in the waters of destruction. It did for me, at least.

People will judge you, especially some *Christians*, because you will fall short and fail to live up to their expectations of you. You may get to the point of cursing God because that is Satan's ultimate plan for every Christian. He is good at what he does; however, God is much better.

While it may not seem like God hears or sees us in the *yuck* of our lives, take heart, because He does. It may feel like He is a million miles away. You may start to wonder why He just will not provide a supernatural healing for the shattered pieces of your heart. You will likely feel that He is out of reach and that He cannot possibly understand what this thorn in your flesh feels like. He does. His ways are not our ways, and our ways are not His ways (Isaiah 55:8–9).

Do not try to make sense of the pain. There will always be questions and what-ifs swirling around in our minds. God may choose to never reveal the answers we desperately seek. We may not understand why something has happened until we cross over the river Jordan and jump into the arms of Jesus for eternity. If we understood life, we would not have any need to demonstrate faith. Faith comes by hearing, not necessarily by seeing (Romans 10:17). That concept is very hard to accept in the face of a storm.

Now in saying that, I certainly wish faith came by seeing, as I am a visual person. It is very hard for my brain to comprehend something if I do not see it played out before me. I guess I am more like the doubting Thomas than any other person in the Bible because my mind needs proof. All the training I have received in my career field shouts that *evidence* is the required piece to make anything real. Yes, I am a doubting Thomas because I crave proof, evidence.

I also struggle with the fact that I cannot have a real verbal conversation with God. Yes, He hears me, but I cannot hear Him audibly like I can when I have a conversation with another person. Yes, He tends to speak through a still small voice (1 Kings 19:11–13). However, life gets loud. My mind, my thoughts become chaotic with the busyness of each day. In fact, my mind tends to be my own worst enemy—right next to Satan.

My learning style requires a real hands-on experience for me to fully understand anything. So then, why does God not just yell louder and make His presence known among the chaos? I wish the good Lord would ride His white horse down from heaven and just hold me in a hug, just so I know He still loves me despite my past and despite my way of thinking.

The sharp truth I have had to just accept is that grace is not a hands-on experience. It is a heart experience. God shows us grace even when our five senses are not engaged or do not understand it. He works in mysterious ways like that.

Journal Entry

Count It All Joy

Count it all joy when you walk through the fire.
(James 1:2)

It is a verse I have read numerous times and probably even had memorized since I could talk. Life brings about trials and heartaches on what seems to be every turn. So far, though battered and bruised at times, by God's grace, I have been more than a conqueror on the journey. Why is it such a hard verse to live out? Perhaps it is simply my utter disdain of the situation. Or maybe it is simply my fear of failure, inadequacy, or living a miserable existence, whether temporary or long-term. Nonetheless, I struggle to count anything joy when it has the potential to burn me and leave me with lasting scars.

As I have muddled through the dark valley of my latest trial—being a police officer who turned into a rape victim at the hands of another officer—I have faced an array of emotions that could probably have me placed in a mental health facility. Only my closest friends know the truth behind my pain. It is my closest friends who hear of my sorrow repeatedly as if I am running in circles on a hamster wheel. They know of the sincere heartbreak that I have fought with for months now. They have seen the tears I have cried on more occasions than I care to count or remember. They have seen the weight loss, the lack of desire to even remove my body from my bed. They have taken note of the anger that has built up around my heart. They have quietly noticed the dark bags that have taken up residence under my eyes because of continuous restless sleep filled with violent nightmares of more rapes. A few have even seen small lacerations and scars pop up from cutting my body. Since they have not gone through my exact trial, they are unable to relate to me in my trial, which, at times, brings about its own issues. Yet for the most part, they try their best to help me cope with being a rape victim, and for that, I am truly thankful. Count it all joy, right?

Before the rapes started, I had an extremely enjoyable career. Being a police officer was one adrenaline rush after another. Some calls brought fear, but for the most part, it was just exciting. I learned a lot about human nature. I have an assortment of stories I could pick from.

It was easy to count it all joy as I walked through those days because life was fun and those fires belonged to other people. Although my career called for me to put out those fires, I did not have to worry about the ramifications and heartbreak of each trial because it was not my personal battle to fight. Sure, I felt empathy and sorrow for them, but in the end, they were not mine to deal with. It is always easy to shed perspective, which was usually just my two cents wrapped in a pretty little bow, because at the end of the shift, I could leave their problems with them and head to my own happy little life.

As I think back to those times, I realize just how much I miss it! However, there are a few things I do not miss. I do not miss the politics of the job nor the constant utter dismay of what I would see each shift. I do not miss the moments in which I could not solve their problems. I especially do not miss the way the agency treated the female officers, including the way they would treat them after being a victim of a crime! I do miss the smiles, sentimental words, and tears of joy I would occasionally come across when I did make a difference for someone. Count it all joy, right? I miss being the "hero" in the moment. I truly miss coming in to help them battle their blaze even just for a few minutes. I deeply miss my life as a police officer.

The count-it-all-joy attitude has faded now because I had to hang up my gun and badge for the last time a few months back due to my own intense fire flaring up. I was raped by a supervisor at the agency, and it was me who was treated badly after I reported it.

As I try to cope with this now, former area partners and law enforcement friends (which are few and far between now that I am out of it and now that my story had spread like a wildfire) tell me that I am "blessed" to have gotten out of the career when I did. Not blessed because I survived each shift (although I was highly blessed in that matter) but blessed because I no longer had to deal with the political agendas and rigid drama of the agency. "Blessed" because I did not experience as much heartbreak as they had in their long lustrous careers (if only they knew). "Blessed" because I did not have the opportunity to become hardened and miserable like them. "Blessed" because they hate their own existence because of the career. "Blessed" because—the list can go on.

Despite my short time there, I did experience a lot when I wore the uniform. I responded to almost every crime possible during my shifts. I experienced probably what most females experience while wearing the same uniform. I did not have to experience these things within the community. I, unfortunately, experienced things within the agency that most of the men never had to. Unjust things. Unfair treatment. Criminal activity against my body. I was raped by a police supervisor and then targeted by the agency until I was forced to resign after I reported it.

How blessed was I, after all? How blessed were the other women I worked with who also experienced traumatic sexual harassment even while

I worked with them? How many other females everywhere experience the same thing because we chose to step into a male-dominated career field? How many other females are forced to resign or are targeted by male officers, sexually harassed, and then forgotten about because they tried to speak of the injustice and corruption within their agency? How are any of these circumstances a blessing?

While I can see what those officers mean, their words still cut deep. Although I am a rape victim (survivor) as well as a highly mistreated female, I still miss my calling of being a police officer. I question if those officers really realize what they are saying to this very young police officer who had many dreams and years ahead of her within that career, if only I had not been...

I listen to them rant their frustrations to me. I hear them express that being in law enforcement for as long as I have been alive has become the very bane of their existence and the truest hatred of their lives. I become envious that they were able to safely experience many years of accomplishing their lifelong dreams of law enforcement while I only had a very short time there. I am jealous that they had the safety of the agency because of their gender. They are merely trying to keep me safe and protected, but how am I supposed to count it all joy when my dream has been shattered because of a fellow police officer that took advantage of me? Where was my safety from the agency?

I am walking through the fire for sure. Instead of joy, I have sorrow for what I lost. I have anger at the agency and the corruption therein. I have envy for those who still can live out my dream no matter how blessed they think I am for getting out of it when I did. If only they knew and understood *my short law enforcement journey. Even still, would they see how my heart misses the career and how it longs to wear the uniform again?*

I guess I should be thankful for the time I did serve as an officer. Some people never get the opportunity to realize their dreams. While the wound is still very fresh and real, I do have regrets. I have tears. I have heartache. I have anger at an agency that did not protect me. I do not find that I have much joy because I no longer have a clear understanding and prospective of my journey or the path that lies ahead of me.

Perhaps one day I will be able to look back and see just how blessed I really was to have gotten out of that career when I did. Maybe I will understand why God chose to remove me from that path just when He did. Maybe it will be revealed to me just why I was raped during that time. Hopefully I will be able to piece together the purpose for the pain. For now, the fire still rages, and my joy has become just a mere pile of ash. Hopefully in time, my purpose on the journey (especially all the fires) will be revealed, the fire extinguished, and my joy restored once again.

Journal Entry

Humpty-Dumpty

Humpty Dumpty sat on a wall,
Humpty Dumpty had a great fall.
All the king's horses and all the king's men,
Could not put Humpty back together again. (Author unknown)

People see me as broken. Not in the physical sense, because although I am getting older, all my physical features are still intact. It may take me three tries to get up off the couch, but I still sleep with my teeth, and I can usually make it to the bathroom before my bladder springs a leak. Yes, I am still in all the right places in my physical body, thankfully.

Yet people tell me that I need to be "fixed." I feel a lot like Humpty-Dumpty. He was noticeably broken. He could not be fixed by the world around him, especially since it was the world that broke him. All the king's horses and all the king's men could not fix him either. As hard as they tried, Humpty-Dumpty remained broken.

Although I am not physically broken, I am emotionally crippled. My spirit rests in a thousand pieces. I do not try to hide it anymore because there is no use. I have been honest with all those I care to be honest with, and they usually accept me just as I am. They let me cry and scream, because although they know that I am broken in this season, they also remind me that I am beautiful and loved.

I still need to be fixed, and there are some out there who frequently remind me—and others—of that. They talk down to me. Their eyes penetrate mine like I am the saddest, sorriest little thing in the world. They *speak about me and my situation to others like I am not even in the same room as them. They judge me. They blame me. They periodically treat me like Humpty-Dumpty because of my messy life.*

Does it make them feel better about their own broken lives? Maybe. However, it hurts my spirit more knowing that they would rather judge my thousand pieces instead of grabbing the superglue to help me piece them back together again.

I may be Humpty-Dumpty in this season of life, but I have a King who will put me back together again. For His healing cannot fail! He does not constantly remind me of my brokenness. He simply picks up each piece and holds them in the palm of His hand. For that is where true healing comes.

Maybe I do need to be fixed. Maybe I am an awful lot like Humpty-Dumpty. The road has been long. The journey has been bumpy, and my armor does have some cracks. Lots of them. However, I am going to let others see my brokenness so they can see where true healing comes from, whenever that happens. My scars show that life has been hard, but they also show that I am a survivor. I will proudly display my cracks for others to see because through my cracks is how the light (Jesus) gets out!

Humpty Dumpty sat on a wall...
Humpty Dumpty had a great fall...
Of all the horses and all the men,
Only the king could put him together again.

Journal Entry

To Everything There Is a Season

To everything there is a season, right? Even the season of sleeping? Of grief? Of sadness? The seasons I am experiencing in my own life right now. Perhaps it is because I am trying to bury away the memories of the last year.

It could be because I really am just depressed like my friends and my counselor keeps saying. Or maybe it is the medication I am on that seems to keep me in bed at all hours. No matter what the reason, I do sleep and cry a lot!

Out of the 168 hours we are given each week, I am probably only out of my bed approximately 40 hours, and even that is pushing it. I just cannot get past the memories of the last year. It seems like even sleeping brings them up with violent nightmares that comes in with a vengeance. However, sleeping dulls the pain more than staying awake in a world of constant reminders of my journey.

So many people ask me why I did not do things differently. Why when I was being assaulted repeatedly, I could not bite him or pick up his gun and shoot him. They ask me why I could not fight him off, especially since I was a police officer. People seem to have their own perspective on what they would have done differently in this situation; however, they do not truly understand what it is like if they have never experienced it before.

Looking back, I wish I could have done one thousand things differently. I wish I could have fought harder or yelled louder. I wish I could have spoken up sooner and not been so afraid. I wish I could have seen the signs that this was looming. I completely missed them. All of them, because of my innocent naivete. The truth is, we all would have done something differently. None of us truly know what we would do until we are in the situation ourselves. Even still, every assault is different to every person, just as the response to it will be too.

When asked why I did not do things in a different way to save myself, I feel utter shame. My answer is because I felt completely powerless. Powerless to his strength. Powerless to my weakness. Powerless to the pain. Powerless to what was happening to me. Powerless to the shame I felt in those moments and afterward. Powerless to the reality that this was now my story. Powerless because of his authority within the agency. I am now just another statistic with no name. Powerless, utter helplessness to perhaps one of the most demeaning situations a person could ever endure.

The season of powerlessness led to the season of constant sleeping. The season of powerlessness also led to the season of depression. Of nightmares. Of an eating disorder. Of more powerlessness and hatred for myself and everyone who was involved in this.

My seasons of laughing and dancing are over for now. I do not know when I will get them back at this point. This is my season. I do not understand it, nor do I like it. I truly wish those around me would at least attempt to understand and accept this time. I guess my season of sleeping can be explained like this: it is like an alcoholic's incessant drinking; they likely drink to dull pain away. I guess I sleep to remove my pain. Either way, this is my season of grief. It cannot be rushed.

Healing may come through a million zzzs, or perhaps it will come through the forty-ish hours of sunlight that I see in a week. Some of those hours see me in counseling. Some see me in church to relearn to fall in love with

God again and to beg Him to love me despite my story. Perhaps this is where my help comes from.

Some hours, although very few, are spent at the homes of very dear friends who do their best to help me try to forget my recent past. The remainder of those hours find me at work trying to keep my mind clear of the constant thoughts of failure that play on repeat. This is my season of grief. My season of crying. My season of mourning. My season of grieving for the piece of my life that was taken from me. It will eventually be my season of healing too.

This is a season to help me grow into a strength that I never knew I had. It will not last forever. Today I may be a caterpillar hiding under the covers and safety of my blankets, but tomorrow, tomorrow I could be a beautiful butterfly soaring above the world with beauty and grace.

> To everything there is a season, and a time to every purpose under the heaven: A time to be born, and a time to die; a time to plant, and a time to pluck up that which is planted; A time to kill, and a time to heal; A time to break down, and a time to build up; A time to weep, and a time to laugh; a time to mourn, and a time to dance; A time to cast away stones, and a time to gather stones together; A time to embrace, and a time to refrain from embracing; A time to get, and a time to lose; A time to keep, and a time to cast away; A time to rend, and a time to sew; A time to keep silence, and a time to speak; A time to love, and a time to hate; a time of war, and a time of peace. (Ecclesiastes 3:1–8 KJV)

I will eventually get back to all the happy seasons of life again. For now, God gives me permission to break down, mourn, and weep. Even Jesus did this in the garden when He begged God to take this cup from Him (Luke 22:42). God does not condemn me for being in this solemn season because He said that there is a season for that too.

Help me. Love me. Care for me. Comfort me. Please do not get mad at me because I sleep so much or cry or even shut down. Do not lose your patience with me because I may be neglecting our friendship or because I may talk in circles and weep over the same issues each day. Please, please do not walk out of my life when I am not what I should be. For this too shall pass. Help me grow. Help me learn to trust. Help me understand what it is to love and be loved once again. Just help me become me, the me I used to be.

When you come across someone amid the season of sadness and loss, just love the person. Be there to provide them the listening ear they may need. Do not judge them. Do not tell them what you think is best for them. Do not tell them how they "should" have responded to the situation. Do not even tell them to stop spending so much time in bed. It is their season to work through. This, too, shall pass.

This season should allow for love, patience, and help to abide. For things grow best in the valley. The soil is prepared to allow a bulb to grow and bloom into a beautiful life. Things are also refined in the fire. Gold, which is a precious metal, must be heated through intense fire before its impurities will be burned out to reveal a pure shiny gold nugget. This season is a necessary process to wholeness.

Powerless to powerful, but it is a process. To everything, there is a season.

Journal Entry
Silence in the Pews

Often, we come to church and hear messages on fear, tithing, sowing and reaping, and faith, but we never open the stage for pure realness. We never approach, or often refuse, some subjects because they almost seem to taboo to talk about in church. Subjects like sexual abuse, domestic violence, and pornography. We remain silent on such issues to avoid creating ripples in the waves or controversy in the pews. For never shall we ever ruffle some feathers or even offend God.

Silence from the pulpit causes silence in the pews. Silence in the pews causes people to suffer unimaginably because they do not feel as if they can talk about their experiences, their struggles, their biggest points of shame. Sadly, then we have many people left hurting because they must carry their burden alone, behind the mask of Christianity. There is no rest for the weary. We should be a church that is more than willing to carry a burden and shoulder life's greatest pain together. So why not start today?

I am a Christian, and I was raped.

I feel like my story is bigger than just my church small group. I feel like this is a major problem in our churches today, but nobody is willing to talk about it because it seems almost taboo. It is not just rape or sexual abuse. It is also things like pornography, drug and alcohol abuse, domestic violence, suicide, etc. too. We hide subjects like this so much because maybe we are afraid to cause ripples in the waves. Perhaps we are concerned that the tithes and offerings will decrease if we step on toes.

Silence from the pulpits causes silence in the pews. Silence in the pews causes people to suffer unimaginably because they feel like they are alone and are not worthy of the help they need. They feel as if they must shoulder their burden by themselves and then hide behind a mask. The reality is, there are so many others sitting right next to them with the same stories, but because there is so much silence, we will never know. It is time to break the silence. It is time to help others understand that it is okay to approach subjects like this in church because they are a part of our stories, and God so desperately longs to give us the healing we need.

I was raped. That is very shameful for me. I feel absolutely disgusting about it! Who else struggles with this that could find healing from just one person being vulnerably willing to talk about their baggage, their messy life?

People with stories like mine, addictions to pornography, drugs, and alcohol, domestic violence need to know that they are not alone. They need to be reminded that they are loved and that the church is a haven of rest to come for healing and accountability.

So many people deal with these issues and more daily. So why is the local church not doing more to reach out to them and tell them that God wants them to come just as they are? As a body of Christ, we need to band together with issues like this so people do not have to feel like they must fight alone. There is refuge in the Savior.

How many hurting people sit silently in the pews each Sunday because they do not feel like they can talk about their experiences? How much suffering comes and goes through the church doors each week? I understand that the church is not a rehabilitation facility, but there is available in it the ultimate healing, love, and accountability if we just have those difficult conversations. We, the church, simply need to be willing to listen to our brothers and sisters and allow them to come forward just as they are, with their pain and questions. This is what it means to "bear one another's burdens" (Galatians 6:2).

Journal Entry

When Time Stood Still

While this entry may be difficult to read, it is important to highlight that Hollywood does not always accurately depict rape. Rape does not always include weapons and intense physical violence, although rape is always violent. It is not always carried out by a perfect stranger who just committed a string of other crimes. Hollywood rarely shows that rape is simply saying no and being disregarded. Yet, it is still rape.

Because of this, I struggled for a long time to believe that what I experienced was, in fact, rape. I knew it was as it was textbook. However, I felt insignificant because mine looked different than what is usually portrayed in the movies. Yet, it was still rape. Whether someone is pointing a weapon at you during the act, or they are just not listening as you say no, it is still rape, and it is a crime.

Reader discretion is advised.

> Time: *A non-spatial continuum in which events occur in apparently irreversible succession from the past through the present to the future; An appointed or fated moment.* (The Free Dictionary)

For the longest time, I hid. I hid from life. From family. From friends. From the reality of my new story on this journey. From the memories of when time stood still for me.

Perhaps it was my ego causing me to hide because I was afraid of what others would think. I was afraid of how I would be labeled, or perhaps it was simply my fear that kept me under cover. I have heard it said that God gives His hardest battles to His strongest soldiers. So it is time to shed the scales from my eyes and face the reality of my story. It is time to remove the glue from my lips and share with others of the atrocities that happened to me, a police officer. No, I will never disclose the name of the person or the agency involved because that is not what matters. The truth is this crime happens everywhere. It is time to move past being just another statistic with no name. It is time to share of when time stood still for me.

In the few times that I have shared my story, I have heard different responses from others. Some told me my story empowered them to change something amiss in their own lives. Others walked away questioning how I could be raped so many times, especially as a police officer by a police officer. Then there were others still who only wanted to know the nitty-gritty details of the moments so they could judge me or use my story against me in some way or, worse yet, gossip about me.

Some blamed me. Some walked away from my life for good, while others flocked to me to share of the encouragement they received from my story. Some told me that I staged the rapes! Some told me I simply had an affair with a married man and had to cover my tracks somehow when I lost my job because of it. Yet then there were those few who reminded me just how loved I was. A few people cried when they heard the news. Then there were those who wanted to "handle" my assailant for me. It has been an array of emotions from my friends, family, and naysayers alike. Much like my own emotions I have experienced along the journey.

While I cannot share everything about my rapes because I refuse to revictimize myself and others who may one day read this, I will share a few details that are important. A few details of the moments when time stood still. A few details that are rarely depicted in the movies.

To say that I am like a child when it comes to the discussion of sex, and anything related to it, would be an understatement. A major understatement. My mother never talked to me about sex because the topic never came up. I also think it was her way of protecting me by keeping that a hidden topic. I was always too involved in school and athletics to worry about whether a boy liked me or not. I was usually too interested in church and God to know that something besides sleeping could, in fact, go on in the bedroom. I was too naive. I guess the subject never needed to come up back then, though. I was a child, unsullied by the world, even well into my adult years.

When I took my position in the police department world, I never realized that I would have to protect myself against my own brothers in blue. I did not understand their profound knowledge of things like grooming and manipulation. I did not know I needed to be on my guard with the very people who swore to protect and serve. When a supervisor started his grooming tactics with me, I did not realize what he was doing. I did not see his ill-intentions coming. I could not see the danger looming because of the childlike innocence within me. This happened in many places, including the office and in the field after calls and not just in a bedroom.

Many times, I found myself fighting against my assailant. He would pick me up or drag my deadweight body into a room while laughing as we went. He was laughing, not me. He would push me or throw me onto the bed like I was a duffel bag waiting to be unpacked. I tried to fight against him, but I was too small for his amount of power.

He grabbed my clothing and tried to yank them off my stiff body. I would pull my shorts back up to shield myself. I would hold my shirt down so he could not see what nobody else had ever seen before. All my efforts failed. I was not strong enough to fend him off. He would laugh out words like, "I am not leaving until I see." When utter exhaustion finally filled every fiber of my being, he would succeed in removing my clothing—every time. He knew he only had to wrestle against my weak body for a short time and then wait me out for me to collapse in sheer fatigue before he could get what he wanted.

With my clothing off and bruises left behind on my arms from fighting so hard, my bare body lay there exposed. It was his "playground" because he knew he was able to overpower me, even with just the silent threat of his service weapon laying nearby. His actions would cause me to cry, feel ill, and be injured internally.

With an ounce of a second wind, I would pull my body away from him and hide to save what little dignity I had left. No matter how far away I got, his strong arms would grab me and pull me back into his grasp. He would continue to become harsher with the assaults. I could not get away from him.

I was in pain. I had never had sex before. I was a virgin. An innocent virgin. The pain was intense. Every time. I pleaded with him to stop. Many times. Every time. He ignored my cries.

He repeatedly forced himself on me in every way he possibly could. When he was finished with one sexual act, he would begin another. Insensitive and unfeeling, he would continue in his barrage, leaving me in pain, shame, and shock. I was powerless to stop it because of his strength and sheer determination to get what only he wanted.

He would hold me down, leaving bruises on my arms. I was so tired of fighting against him, but he kept going sometimes until I bled or cried. The pain was harsh. Intense. Like no pain I had ever known before because I was not ready.

When he was done, he would get dressed and leave like nothing happened. He warned me to never tell anyone. Every time. I was then faced with the task of going to work with my sore body and collapsed emotions in which I had to hide.

Even at work, he would grab my body and pull it into his. Nobody was around. There were no cameras. He would grope me on the outside of my uniform as my stiff body could only sit motionless with fear. He would pull me in and put his hands under my clothing even with all the equipment I was wearing. I would fold my body while grabbing his hands to stop him. There was no stopping him. Ever.

He would constantly remind me of his power around the police station. He was my supervisor and high up on the food chain at that. No matter how hard I tried, I could never win. No matter how much I wanted to cry out of the atrocities he committed against me, he kept me trembling in fear. So I remained silent. For months. Suffering in unimaginable pain. Alone.

To make things worse, he was usually on duty and always armed during the rapes. Although he never threatened to use it, his gun was always only inches away from me. It was as if he was using that tactic as a silent threat to get what he wanted.

He would rape me as I listened to the police radio while he was the watch commander on duty. To drown out the pain or to disassociate, as it is called in the mental health world, when I could no longer fight, I would listen to the calls on the radio. A missing child, a concrete truck that just spilled his load on the street, dispatchers calling out to this person violating me for his supervisory assistance while he ignored them. Listening to the radio did not change the circumstances of what he was doing to my body, but at least it helped my mind go to another place, to another person's battle while my body was being taken advantage of in the most demeaning way possible.

Finally, it was on a cold winter day when he came to rape me for the last time. He was there for a purpose: to keep me quiet from talking to the authorities. He ignored my no and raped me once again.

It was after that rape when I finally found the courage within me to end his "game" and talk to the police (ironically my own team that did not seem to care). He would never be able to hurt me again because I finally found my courage, my voice, to fight against him. I had to stop him from hurting me or any other female again. I am convinced he had other victims too.

To this day, my assailant has never been arrested. The State Attorney's Office chose not to file charges against him. They said it was due to a lack of evidence and inconsistencies in the complaint. However, I will always believe it was so they could fulfill their own political agenda due to his position within the community and stature of the police department standing behind him. He was allowed to retire from the police department while I was forced to resign months before the last rape because of my initial complaint of rape. I imagine he probably lives a life of paradise today, while I am in a proverbial prison of his making.

Time continues to stand still for me daily as I am somehow reminded of something that happened on those fateful days. He changed me as a person all because of his selfish desires. To add salt to the wound, he will never have to pay for his crime because I could not convince anyone enough of his dishonest personality, masterful manipulation, and grooming tactics. It was me who was blackballed by the agency, unable to get another job in law enforcement again. The only positive thing to come from this nightmare is that he is no longer in a position of authority at a prominent police department. As much as I wish he was in jail for his senseless crime, and the agency was held accountable for their caustic role in the matter, at least I can rest, even among the nightmares, knowing that he can never do this again to another female there. Unfortunately, he can still work at a police department if he so chooses because he still holds his police certification. Nothing was taken from him, just from me.

So there it is. Just a fraction of my story in black and white for everyone to see and to possibly judge. It is part of my journey now. An appointed or fated moment of when time stood still for me.

To everything there is a season and a time to every purpose under the heaven. (Ecclesiastes 3:1)

At least this is what I am choosing to believe now.

Journal Entry

Intimate Connection

He took the most intimate piece of my soul without hesitation. Without my permission. He took my virginity. He was the first man intimately inside my body. He stole it. Just like that.

Whether I wanted it or not, I now have a connection with a man who never cared one iota about me. He only cared to fulfill his need at the time, and he did so at my expense.

He was the first person to know what the inside of my body felt like. As painful as it was, he was the first person to show me what it felt like to have someone inside of me too. He was the first person to make that intimate connection with my heart and soul. It was not love. It was not wanted. He did not have permission to attach himself like he did. He placed his body in the forbidden places of mine in which he was not allowed to go. He was never supposed to know me like that. Even though those moments are long over now, and he has probably moved on to another female, I will always have this unwanted memory with him.

As forced as it was, he was my first sexual encounter. I cannot change that now. So I am left with these feelings of inadequacy and unfulfilled desire because he stole what was not his to take, like a thief in the night. Just like that.

He left me in the state of shock, not quite sure of what had just happened. How could that happen to me? I am not above anything, and I know that. Yet how did that happen to me, a police officer? How did he do this to me? I did not give it to him. I did not want him to have it. Now I am left with *this intimate connection and trauma bond with a groomer and a manipulator who very much abused his power over me.*

How is that possible? It makes me feel even more disgusting as a human being, because how can anyone miss something that wounded them so deeply? It seems inconceivable yet confusing at the same time.

I think of his family. His kids. His wife, another person whom he has known on the same intimate level as me. Perhaps the only difference is that their intimacy was actually filled with love for one another. How does she feel knowing that her beloved forcefully took another woman? Perhaps more than one woman, as there may be other victims. Is she wounded too? Has she cried many of her nights away as I have? Was she in shock when she heard the news of her husband's misbehavior? What does her heart feel? Broken? Wounded? Misplaced? Abandoned, disregarded, or betrayed? Or maybe he has convinced her that there was a mix-up or that I am a liar. I am not sure of her feelings, but I wish I could hug her and tell her that I am sorry for the anguish his actions have caused at least two families—his and mine. He made the mistake, so why do I feel like I need to ask her for forgiveness?

Why do I miss something that I never wanted or even asked for? Perhaps I just miss the piece of my soul that was taken from me, and knowing that he has it makes me long to have it back again. It rests with him forever now. I find that it is not him that I miss but the intimate part of me that was stolen that I can never get back again.

CHAPTER 6

While it has been many years since this dark time in my life, I will always be actively healing from it so as not to fall back into the array of emotions I experienced from those very dark days. I will continue to learn about sexual assault and the psychology behind it so I can understand my own baggage. I am also hopeful that my scars will aid others in working through their own trauma.

For the longest time, I judged myself, just as everyone else did after they learned that the assaults kept happening to me. I did not understand it. I knew I was too afraid to speak up because of who my perpetrator was, but how does anyone *let* that happen repeatedly? The reality is that I did not *let* that happen. There was a silent form of psychological manipulation called *trauma bonding* occurring during each violation. This is a concept that makes perfect sense to me now as I look back on the trauma.

While I am not a psychologist or a therapist in any way, I have done some research on many psychological topics to try to understand what happened to me. I also completed a graduate program on crisis response and trauma, which has shed much light on traumatic experiences. I also put in much time and hard work with my therapist over the years to heal from my past.

The concept of trauma bonding was created many years ago by two psychologists from Canada and was eventually coined by Patrick Carnes, PhD, in 1997. Trauma bonding is, in essence, forming an emotional attachment to the person who hurt you. It is defined in the book *Psychiatric and Mental Health Nursing for Canadian Practice*

(2010) as "a strong emotional attachment between an abused person and his or her abuser, formed as a result of the cycle of violence." It is a trauma response that occurs when our brains are looking for a way to survive. It is very common for victims of sexual abuse, domestic violence, human trafficking, etc. to form a trauma bond with their abuser.

A trauma bond requires two components: a power imbalance and intermittent reinforcement. In my scenario, both were always present. He was my supervisor, and I was his subordinate (power imbalance). He made promises to not do this again, to make sure I was "safe" at work, to keep being my "friend," etc., followed by threats about my job and safety should I talk, including silent threats with his weapon lying nearby as he violated me (intermittent reinforcement). By doing this, he maintained a tight control over my mind and emotions, which kept me in fear of reporting this and him in control over my body and mind.

Because of this *bond*, I cared deeply about how talking about this would negatively affect his family, which is why I had the hardest time reporting his behaviors. He made me feel guilty about what he was doing to me because he had a family. He convinced me that nobody would believe me if I spoke up because he was "powerful" at the agency. While I knew it was rape, and he knew it too, my brain tried to make excuses for his behaviors because he convinced me that I somehow *wanted* what he was doing to my body. He controlled my mind into believing that I would only be *safe* with him because of what he was doing *for* me. The reality is that what he was doing was sexual assault because I said no, and I kept saying no during each violation. I felt powerless to stop his actions because of the psychological manipulation behind his deeds.

In essence, I felt *sympathy* for him as he continually hurt my body because that was his tactic to keep me quiet. Even though he was hurting me, he made me feel bad about turning him in. Initially, I did not want him to get in trouble for his behavior because I felt that I would be in trouble too—by him, by my agency—because he convinced me I would be, even though I did not do anything wrong in the first place. Ironically, however, I was in *trouble* each time he hurt my body, soul, spirit, and mind with the masterful manipulation.

I now understand more about my response to the trauma and why it kept occurring for several months before I was able to finally break free of this traumatic cycle. None of it made sense to me when I was *in* the battle. It was not until years later that I was able to see with clearer eyes what was actually happening to everything about me during this time in my life.

Trauma bonding—while may still be difficult to understand if one has not experienced it firsthand, it is real. Perhaps a little more care, compassion, and research is in order instead of immediately judging and blaming a victim for their response, which is what I experienced from many people, including the police department. Psychological manipulation/control is very powerful, and it is very difficult to break away from.

Journal Entry

Reflect

I look into the mirror and see my eyes penetrating back at me. They are filled with anger and hurt like no other eyes I have seen before. They are police officer eyes. They are victim eyes. They are covered in mistrust and doubt for the unseen beautiful person that stares back. They long to be loved by a true love and not a stolen lust. My eyes tell a story, a story of a simple girl behind her badge. My story.

Yesterday, I was an innocent and naive little girl. Today, though, today I am a hardened old woman with a story filled with wounds and regret. My worries show in the lines displayed across my newly aged face.

I feel like a paper-mache doll who is constantly being layered up with life's hardest lessons and battles. One layer is fear. The next is frustration. The next one is perhaps the desire to fit somewhere. Then there is the layer where I am told that I am not pretty enough. Or loved enough. Or cherished whatsoever. I am reminded that I am a failure. A loser. A misfit. Then there are other layers still of the senseless tragedies I responded to when I wore the badge. Death. Injury. Forlorn people. A lot like myself. The layers keep piling on reminding me that I am just a fake hiding under the weight of problems. Perhaps I need some rain to come and wash the layers off and give me a fresh start. A clean slate. A new prospective.

I see what nobody else sees. I am my biggest and worst critic as I stare at the face in the mirror. I often wonder where my innocence has gone and why it disappeared so quickly.

I think to myself, Is the face that I see in the mirror the one I want others to see? No. Not at all. Not that face. Because the face that I see in the mirror is a lie. A failure. A misfit. A grieving and broken person and former police officer. Why would I want others to know and experience—well, me? I am afraid I would simply scare them away.

I recently went to a women's event at a church called Reflect. I went to that one-night conference just moments after I started writing this piece. How ironic as that conference was unknowingly about looking in the mirror. They even gave us a little gift of a compact mirror to remind us to reflect on God in our lives. Everywhere we go, to remind us of our inner beauty.

The conference was powerful. Just me and seven thousand other women packed in rooms across the United States.

The truth is that the face that I see in the mirror is a face that is so loved by God. I can shed the mask and come just as I am. No matter how many times I have failed in this life or how many times I have let myself down, God is proud of me. No matter how many times I have been hurt by the actions of others, God tells me to come, and He will give me rest. He reminds me that His eye is on the sparrow so I can also know that He watches over me too. God tells me that I am beautiful even when my situation screams otherwise. God created me; my situation did not, so I should probably listen to Him.

God loves me. He also likes me too! He enjoys being in my presence, and He wants me to enjoy being in His presence as well. He does not see what I see staring back at me in the mirror. He sees beauty and love. He sees grace and mercy. He sees forgiveness through the cross. He sees a special creation specifically handcrafted into the image of His Son. He does not see me as a wounded police officer or a failure. He does not see me as a problem child or rebellious misfit. He does not see me as a rape victim or a statistic with no name. He does not even see me as a forlorn loser like I tend to see myself sometimes. He sees me with His perfect eyes. He does not lust for me like a police officer once did. God longs for me so that He can love me like the perfect Father that He is.

When I look in the mirror and see something about myself that I do not like, I am merely saying that God has made a mistake. God makes no mistakes. I have simply lost my contentedness in the Creator!

Is the face that I see in the mirror the one I want others to see? Not yet. God is still crafting His masterpiece. He is masterfully sanding off the rough edges of insecurities and mistrusts. He is hammering off the rape victim status to make way for His healing. He is painting me with His beautiful promises that I will not see in my own mirror. He is polishing His diamond in the rough that has been hidden for so many years. He is preparing me to reflect Him to the world on this journey. Although sawdust still lingers in my view, in the mirror of God's eyes, I am perfect!

CHAPTER 7

When the sexual assaults first began, I completely changed, quickly. I was no longer my bubbly self. Instead, I shut down because I did not know how to handle such a grievous situation, especially against a police officer and, subsequently, a whole department. I felt like I needed to fight alone because I was too afraid to speak up and share what that felt like, especially when others might not understand.

On the other hand, I was not in the position to speak up because of who he was and where we worked. I felt trapped. I felt alone. I did not trust God. I did not trust my loved ones. I surely did not trust other police officers during that time. All I could do was suffer in silence to protect myself from the wiles of the devil and the man that hurt me.

I wonder if this was how Jesus felt in the garden, when He begged His Father to take this cup (trial) away from Him (Luke 22:42). I imagine He must have felt alone, too, when nobody else understood His plight. Did He feel betrayed by God for having to pay such a high cost for the souls of men?

I have wondered if Jesus ever struggled with forgiveness toward God because of His brutal death on the cross. Jesus always knew His purpose in life. He was all knowing. He was made perfect in human flesh. He was meant to be a propitiation for all our sins (1 John 2:2). However, His body, soul, and spirit were still gravely wounded by the people of this world, just so He could die for them, for us. Leading up to that point, and even during His brutal crucifixion, did He ever have even the slightest anger toward God for this? Albeit perfect and sinless, He was still also a human being after all. The devil still tried to tempt Him.

The Bible does not say that we cannot be angry. It simply says to be angry and to sin not (Ephesians 4:26). Since Jesus was a perfect being, it is possible that He got angry a time or two, but He never sinned. The Bible even shares of the moment when Jesus, in anger, flipped the tables of the money changers because they, in their sin, made His house a house of thieves rather than of prayer (John 2:15–16). He was broken before His Father about His impending death. The interesting piece is that if He was angry, I think God understood it. I think He understands our anger, our pain, if only we do not sin in the act of expressing it.

Forgiveness is hard. It is hard to understand when you have been hurt so badly. It is even harder to accept when the person who hurt you is not sorry for their actions. It takes time, sometimes a lifetime.

Forgiveness is a daily battle that is sometimes not overcome in our own timeline and ability. Just like the hurt did not happen overnight, the healing may not either. Show yourself a little extra grace as you navigate through the healing and forgiveness process. Some days are better than others. Some moments hold more clarity. Some seconds, in hindsight, make more sense.

I struggle with forgiveness as it does not make sense to me. At all. Especially after someone with authority over you has broken into your world. It may never make sense on how I am supposed to forgive after such an atrocious act.

I believe it is okay to walk through the process of grief for your loss at a slower pace. Trauma is a form of loss. It is perfectly acceptable to cry, scream, and punch the pillow when the memories of your hurt overtake you. Just like physical wounds, emotional and mental wounds take time to heal too.

I have heard many forms of what forgiveness *is* and what it is supposed to look like. Yet very rarely are we reminded of what forgiveness *is not*. What forgiveness is not is also important, as it is a gentle reminder to show yourself extra grace in the healing process.

Forgiveness is not simple.

It is not forgetting.

It is not pretending that the trauma never happened.

Forgiveness is not costless, although harboring the hurt can cost you everything.

Forgiveness is not necessarily accomplished overnight. It is a process. Sometimes a one-step-at-a-time process, and that is perfectly acceptable.

It is also not always just a one-time thing either. Forgiveness may need to happen 490 times over again (Matthew 18:21–22).

Forgiveness is not retaliation.

It is not denial.

It is not dependent on the other person.

Forgiveness is not boundaryless. You can fully forgive someone but still place specific boundaries on the situation. For example, just because you may forgive someone does not mean that you must still include them in your life. That mentality could ultimately just set you up to be hurt again. While not always necessary, it is appropriate and acceptable to set boundaries after a trauma has occurred.

Forgiveness is not motivated solely by guilt.

Forgiveness is not condoning someone else's actions.

Forgiveness does not change the situation, because that situation has already occurred. However, it absolutely will change your perspective in the matter. Forgiveness, or the lack thereof, will ultimately either set you free or hold you captive in a prison of your own making. No matter what forgiveness looks like, it can change everything for your very wounded spirit.

Journal Entry

The Incredible Hulk

Some days I feel like the Incredible Hulk ready to take on the world with my incredible strength and large green arms. Other days, I feel like a fly on the wall whose backside has just been shoved up into her head because she was hit with a newspaper that she did not see coming. Some days, I am ready to face the giants. Other days, I am ready to curl up and, well, run away from home. I am simply ready to give up the fight. I cannot have it both ways, though, and I know that.

I am not even sure what I hope to achieve in this battle or what I would like to see happen anyway. My mind is confused. I just know that I want to see justice somehow.

I want others to believe me that such a man could and did commit a crime against me. I want to be treated with respect and dignity, what little bit I have left. I want to know that my assailant had to pay for his crime instead of living la vida in his permitted retirement. While at the same time, I want to make things safe for other females who dare to step into the police world and live out their dreams. I want the safety for them that I never got.

I am not even sure what the point of this entry is. Perhaps it is just to hear myself talk or write rather. Maybe it is just another way to display my many arrays of emotions and feelings that are expected in the healing process of this season. Maybe it is to express, just once more, how disappointed I am in the "justice" system because they failed greatly as they have done with many other sexual assault cases. Regardless, is babbling on about craving justice and safety for others such a bad thing?

I do not know what justice looks like. I cannot explain it. Yet I will know it when I see it because I will be satisfied when it comes, if it ever does. Perhaps for now, my random musings will show others that it is okay to experience emotion—the good, the bad, and the ugly. Even Jesus wept at one point, and probably more, but only one time was recorded.

Now where are the tissues? Or the punching bag? Or the chocolate? The Incredible Hulkette needs them to combat the newspaper that is looming nearby.

Journal Entry

Badge of Horror

I often remember his badge number because I seem to see it everywhere. While I cannot share those numbers publicly, they are a series of numbers that should have no meaning whatsoever. Yet when put in a certain order, the number becomes the memory of my worst nightmare.

Perhaps one day, his law enforcement identification was a badge of honor found hanging bravely on a decorated uniform. A once honorable police officer wearing this badge of distinction. For me, however, his badge is now just a "badge of horror" when I see his numbers around town.

I cannot seem to get away from those numbers. I seem to see them everywhere I go. At the gas station. On license plates. On the clock every time it hits that time of day. Even on my own identification card at my new job. Worse yet, I still see them around town on a patrol vehicle that I used to work with. I cannot seem to get away from those numbers. I cannot seem to get away from the nightmares of several horrible moments in time. The assaults, by the person who once wore those numbers on his police badge.

Perhaps that is God's gentle reminder to pray for my assailant every time I see them. Prayer is a hard task to complete when I have not even been able to forgive him yet. Maybe it is the devil's "brilliant" tactic to keep me held captive in his grip. Regardless, I cannot help the tension that creeps into my body when I see his police identification somewhere around town. My heart races. My hands shake. My mind relives each moment as if I am still in it. My time stands still. All because of the combination of specific numbers that has just appeared before me somewhere.

Will I ever come to the point where those numbers will not scare me? Will it always feel like three seconds have been taken off my life because of the sheer nervousness that grips me when I see them?

His police identification once stood for greatness for one man. For one man that was never charged with his crime. Now the memories of those numbers—of that man—live to haunt me. To torture me. To make me more afraid than anything else in the world.

Time stopped several times for me all because of one man who abused his badge. His power. His position within the community. Now I am left with the aftermath of his actions. I will eventually rise from the ashes of the memories and proclaim my victory. My victory from fear. My victory from my powerlessness. My victory from my memories. My victory over him.

Journal Entry

10-7 (Out of Service)

A car accident. An intoxicated driver. A smothered baby. A bloody domestic violence scene. A drive-by shooting. A suicide. These are all stories that I can remember from calls I responded to as a police officer. There were many. Many more than what I just listed. Too many to recount. Several of them will be forever seared into my mind never to be forgotten.

I could tell you about the intoxicated pedestrian who walked out in front of an SUV on a dark and busy roadway. That person was struck and killed instantly. I will never forget our efforts to "save" her lifeless body with CPR as the crowds gathered. Nor can I erase the image of her limp Jell-O-like broken bones being picked up by the medical examiner after the investigation was complete.

I could share of the innocent motorcyclist who was run over and dragged down a busy highway by a drunk driver who then fled the scene. I had a conversation with him shortly after I arrived on the scene, just seconds after it happened. He died too. I could express my anger when I arrived at the call where a five-week-old baby had been accidentally smothered to death by her drug-and-alcohol impaired mother as they both slept—in the same bed. Maybe I should mention of the domestic violence call where the victim and the home were both covered in her blood because of an injury to her face that went down to her bones.

I can never forget the suicide where a young father hung himself in his six-year-old daughter's closet, only for his daughter to discover him hanging. I remember the sound of his agonal breathing and watched his bowels release as he lay there dying while his child wept close by. Yes, my stories of my law enforcement career could go on.

Each call, in its own way, was both sad and taxing on the human mind, body, and soul. Very rarely was there a call that put a smile in my heart but instead tears in my eyes. Some days I could not make a difference. Some days I would leave work wondering where God was amid each tragedy. Yet all days, no matter what the call was that I responded to, I was both humbled and thankful to wear my badge. It truly was my honor and a dream come true.

I was just a rookie, but in my city, even the rookies were initiated in quickly. There was no warm-up session. You either made it, or you did not. Our boots hit the ground running, from the moment the shift started until the moment we went 10-7 (out of service) at the end of shift. The calls were numerous and varied. They were all very different from the last one. It was a busy agency. The job itself was exhilarating.

I aided many people in my time as an officer. I treated each person with respect and a certain level of empathy and dignity if I was able to. I was a small female but would step up to the biggest challenge. Sometimes the job absolutely terrified me. Yet I would never allow my fear to show because I was the strength for the person I was helping. Police work was my life, and it was also my greatest love.

I look back at my time as an officer, and I long to have it back again. I greatly miss what I did out on the streets of my town. I was not perfect—no cop ever is—but I tried my best out there. I find that I miss the people. The relationships. The sheer pleasure of knowing that I tried to and sometimes could make a difference for that one person, even if just for the night. Yes, I miss it.

I also find that I miss my career because it was taken away from me for a situation out of my control. I was raped multiple times by a supervisor, and I was the one forced to resign when I finally found the courage to speak up about it. I was the one retaliated against and bullied by other officers after I found a small portion of my voice. I was the one living in absolute fear as I entered the building each shift. I often wonder how many other female officers are in this same fear, for the same reasons.

I was ignored. I was lied to. I was minimized. I was dismissed. Even nearly a year after my forced resignation. I have discovered that I have been blackballed from law enforcement because I stood up for what was right. Right for me. Right for other females and victims in the career field. I was not important enough to be given a fair and impartial investigation because, after all, I was merely the rookie cop fighting against the big dogs. I was a female, which probably did not help the situation because females tend to be highly mistreated in the law enforcement career field.

Perhaps I simply was not corrupt enough to make it as a police officer. Although that is not very fair to say, because there are thousands of truly decent cops in this country. I was not trainable in that matter because I would not play their game. I say that cautiously, too, because of the many genuinely good officers out there who are not corrupt and who do their best each shift just as I tried to do. Yet to think of the corruption that is present and rampant is truly heartbreaking in a career that is supposed to protect and serve others. Especially a career that I was good at and enjoyed before this nightmare occurred.

I do not wear the badge anymore. I morosely clocked my last 10-7 almost a year ago now. It still breaks my heart that I cannot wear my badge.

It shatters me even more every time I get another rejection letter in the mail from another agency.

My dream is over. Sometimes I even find tears slipping from my eyes knowing that. I guess I can rest in the fact that even during the hardest calls, I did make a difference for someone, even if they do not know it. Whether it was in giving them a much-needed hug or simply a "free" ride to jail, I did make a difference. For someone. Maybe, just maybe, they will look back, think of me, and smile as they journey. For now, however, and minus the heartache that I faced in the end, I will always have my memories of my greatest pleasure in this life—serving as a police officer.

Squad car 21 is now grievously 10-7. Godspeed to those remaining on the thin blue line. Go out there and do some good. For me.

CHAPTER 8

One of the first recorded sexual assaults in history was that of Dinah in the Old Testament of the Bible. Dinah was the daughter of Jacob and Leah. While she was likely not allowed to be independent because of her cultural upbringing, she was likely strong and confident in her nature. She was "defiled" (raped) by Shechem when she went into the city to meet with the other women of the land (Genesis 34). Ultimately, her brothers killed Shechem and his family because of his evil deed toward her.

Another early assault written in biblical history was the rape of Tamar in the Old Testament. Tamar was the daughter of King David and the daughter-in-law of Judah, twice. She was not without pain in life as God took her first husband, Er, because he was evil in His sight (Genesis 38:7). God then took her second husband, Onan, because he displeased the Lord by refusing to obey God (Genesis 38:10).

Tamar was not without heartache. She likely felt alone and abandoned because of her losses. To make matters worse for her, her father, King David, was tricked by her half-brother, Amnon, also King David's son, because Amnon *loved* his sister. One day, Amnon pretended to be ill, so he asked his father to send Tamar in to care for him. It was at that time that he *forced* Tamar to lie with him (sexual assault), causing her deep shame and causing him to be a "fool" in Israel (2 Samuel 13). It took time for any justice to prevail for Tamar. Despite this, God never forgot her name.

Another travesty recorded in the Bible was that of Lot and his daughters in Genesis 19. When the angels of the Lord came to

Sodom, Lot begged for them to stay in his home with them. When the wicked people of the city got word of this, they demanded Lot release the men to them so they could have relations with them. Instead, Lot offered his virgin daughters to the wicked people to do to them as they pleased. What father, in his right mind, would ever offer his daughter to be raped by evil men! I just cannot comprehend that.

The story later goes on to say that after Lot and his daughters were pulled to safety from Sodom by those angels, they resided on a mountain outside of Zoar. Because of Lot's age, his daughters were afraid of being alone, so they tricked their father into getting drunk and then went in and lay with him to preserve their seed. Lot was unaware of their pernicious deeds against him.

While, ultimately, God used that situation for His good, why did He allow that to happen in the first place? Perhaps it is not for me to question God's ways, but He had rescued them from a very wicked and sinful city, only for them to wrong their own father. While I do, some may not consider this as a form of sexual assault, but it is wrong, nonetheless, because of the trickery and deceit they used to accomplish their own selfish desires.

Genesis 39 shares some of the story of Joseph. Joseph had a tough childhood, as his own family turned their back on him because of their jealousy of him. Despite the pain, he ended up becoming a very successful man because God was with him.

The Bible describes Joseph as being handsome in form and appearance. His master, Potiphar, found favor in him and made him an overseer of his house. Potiphar's wife quickly took note of this handsome man and demanded day after day that Joseph lie with her. Day after day, Joseph declined her advances.

Finally, one day, Potiphar's wife caught Joseph by his garment and again demanded that he lie with her. Joseph immediately ran out of the house, accidently leaving his garment behind in his haste. Potiphar's wife then concocted a story, called the men of the household, showed them the garment, and accused Joseph of rape. Joseph was thrown into prison for falsely being accused of a crime that he did not commit.

Unfortunately, sexual assault goes back to the very beginning of time because this world is full of sin. Sin does not discriminate. It is a choice within our free will that often leads to others being wounded by our own actions.

How do you forgive what you cannot forget? How do you forgive God for what you cannot forget? How do you trust that He will keep you safe and secure in this life? No weapons formed against us shall prosper (Isaiah 54:17). I find this specifically ironic knowing that my story of sexual assault dealt directly with a police officer and a *justice* system. Their weapons *did* prosper in my mind because I was made to feel that I did not matter to them and by them and by God. How do I forgive them for that?

I struggle to cope with the fact that my mother never got to see me fulfill my career aspirations. She will never be by my side at my wedding. She will never get to welcome any future grandchildren into this world. She was not there to hold me as I wept my days away after the assaults.

The physical act of the crime is over now. The final chapter of my mother's life has been completed for years. Now I must work to heal from the emotional and mental scars left behind. It has not been easy. I still become increasingly angry when I see the police living out my dream because I so desperately want my dream job back or when I think that no charges were brought forth against the man who harmed me.

It is even more grievous to know that the man that tried to destroy me can still be a police officer again if he so chooses. It feels like a small stab to my heart knowing that someone can "protect and serve" and harm others all at the same time. Yet what I have learned is that the pain of the initial trial will not always feel so raw. He no longer has control over me, and she will always be by my side in every way. He cannot hurt me further; her death cannot wound me deeper, unless I continue to allow those traumas to harm my spirit mentally and emotionally. That is my choice.

I will always miss my mother. Initially, my dignity, my confidence, my strength, and my innocent trust in others was stolen away from me. Yet God has a way of healing internally when we are ready to move forward. It is out with the old and in with the new. In Christ, I am a new creation. The old things about my broken spirit have passed away, and it is becoming new once again (2 Corinthians 5:17). It is a process. Weeping may endure for a night, but joy will come in the morning (Psalm 30:5). God can be a light in my path just as He was for Dinah, Tamar, and Joseph (Psalm 119:105) if I give Him permission to illuminate my way and my healing process along the journey.

Journal Entry

Shattered

I got the news today that no victim (survivor) ever wants to hear: the State Attorney's Office will not be filing charges on your case. To say that my heart broke would be an understatement. A massive one! It, in fact, shattered into a million pieces, way beyond repair. Even superglue cannot fix the damage this time.

I probably should have thought more positively with my case. However, the truth is that I knew the day was coming in which I would hear those words simply because of the political aspect of my case. For my assailant was a well-known, high-ranking supervisor of a medium-size police department, with many political powers in its grasp.

The very law broke the law and got past the consequences of the law. So I cannot say that I was surprised at the phone call because I was being prepared throughout the entirety of the case to hear those words. Whether it was the police agency ignoring the issue for five months, as they watched me hit rock bottom before they did anything about it, or whether it was the state department investigating the case who conducted a poor investigation by leaving out key witnesses and facts. Or maybe it was the very insensitive nature of the State Attorney's Office in dealing with me because they were personal friends with my assailant. I will never forget the moment the state attorney assigned to my case called me a liar and threatened to file charges against me in the meeting we had together. As if my already fragile heart did not hurt enough.

Yes, all along, the very people who were supposed to protect me had their own subtle way of telling me that they were not going to do anything about my case. They had and fulfilled their own agenda. They let the bad guy get away and maybe more than once.

As much as I cannot say that I was surprised at the phone call, I still found tears welling up in my eyes as I listened. I felt anger and rage build up in my heart and mind at the injustice I was hearing. A police officer got away with a crime. I wish I had an old-school phone so at least I would have had the satisfaction of slamming it down on its base when I hung up on the state attorney. Yet I did not. So I just cried as I drove down the road with my little, tiny nephew in the back seat.

Another lawbreaker walks free while his scared victim tries to figure out how to survive life now. Another bad guy gets the pleasure of thinking he beat the law because there was not enough evidence or even a fair investigation to convict him. A corrupt police officer gets bragging rights that he won; therefore he can now tell everyone else that his victim was lying the whole time when, in fact, he secretly knows that the truth was spoken during the entire investigation. (I use the term corrupt police officer lightly because most cops are not actually bad people.)

His friends and agency will never hear how his victim was actually telling the truth about his unkempt behavior. They will never hear that he is, in fact, a damaging person hiding behind the mask of police officer. His name is clear now, while the true victim has been thrown into the mud again.

I feel like I can no longer show my face in public anymore. What if I run into him, and I must see the smug look on his face that he won? My safety is compromised because he walks the very streets as I do, and he has the support of a police agency and now the State Attorney's Office.

I cannot trust law enforcement any longer because it was proven just how corrupt the system can be. There is no true justice when you are fighting against a high-ranking police officer.

I will never have my day in court to prove his ill ways and sexual addiction. I will never get to share the pain I felt in each violation. I was not heard—by anyone. My feelings were not accounted for. I was blamed for his crime because he knew how to play the game and the system so well, and they believed him.

I imagine he is probably kicking up his feet, drinking a beverage with his buddies in celebration of a broken system who protected a pernicious individual. All the while, I remain in my bed because I am too crushed and depressed to get out of it.

He won. The suspect won.

Yes, my heart is shattered into a million pieces, way beyond repair. Not even superglue can fix the damage this time.

Journal Entry

Forty-One Pages

My mind is everywhere tonight. It wants to be angry. It has every right to be angry. My spirit is broken. It also has a right to be broken. My heart lacks trust. For everyone. Even those closest to me. It hurts to even say that because I know I have been surrounded with good solid friends and family during this tumultuous season. I am not sure who to trust anymore or who even cares to listen to my rants at this point.

I received the initial police report today. I struggled to keep my sanity as I read through all forty-one pages of it. It was full of lies, mistruths, fabrication, and deception. All because one man denied his actions to make himself look innocent when he was not.

I thought forgiveness for him was starting to come. I will never forget what he did to me. I was almost to the place where I could release my anger toward him and move on, until I read his interview today. Now a whole new set of angry emotions are built up inside of me at the atrocities he said. First, he commits repeated crimes against me, and then he denies it, just like he said he would do if I ever talked. It feels like he got away with murder because he murdered the truth, the circumstances, my career, and nearly my life, all because of his sexual deviance and powerful position.

True justice was not served nor will it ever be. The victim will always look like the bad guy in the matter while the real suspect lives an untouchable life, because he, apparently, is untouchable. By not charging him with a crime (there were many he committed during the violations), the justice (injustice) system verified that.

All my fears were verified through forty-one pages. He lied. He was protected. He got away with it. The sad part is that I am not sure what else there is left for me to do in my feat for justice.

At this point, I have allowed this case to consume me, probably like any true victim would do. I eat, sleep, and think of this case as if it is on replay in my head. Not because I want to remember the painful moments, but because I am still in shock at how minimized this crime has become for me. Not for me, because I can never minimize that, but how others have treated this case and me. I find myself trying to figure out where the true justice is. Because it certainly is not shown within my case. Another criminal walks free, just like 974 others out of 1,000 do in this matter. Some justice.

Perhaps I am just ranting at this point, but I cannot begin to explain the pain in my heart over all of this. Maybe it is time to move on. Yet if I simply dismiss it, like everyone else seems to be doing, then someone else could get hurt down the road by the same callous actions of my assailant. I am struggling to live with myself as it is. I could not imagine the remorse I would feel within my soul if someone else had to go through this because I chose not to keep fighting.

I am angry. Outraged. Hardened by his evil ways and deceptiveness in the matter. How was he successful in his lies? Perhaps I should feel bad for him because his mind is so sick that he thinks he did nothing wrong. Deep down inside, however, I believe he knows exactly what he did.

I am enraged at the justice system's failing "attempt" and lack of concern for the matter, especially with something involving police officers. My demeanor has become quite forlorn because my life does not matter to those who are supposed to protect and serve.

Where is my protection? Where was it during the times I was being assaulted by a cop? Where will it be tomorrow when I walk the very streets as my assailant knowing he is a free man?

Forty-one pages of utter lies, deception, and corruption by one man has ruined my life and defeated my spirit. Forty-one pages, that is all it took.

Forgive me, but I am going to cry my eyes out now.

Journal Entry

Sticks and Stones

> Sticks and stones may break my bones, but words will never hurt me. (Unknown)

I found myself drawn to the forty-one pages yet again, as I lay awake throughout the night, for the one-hundredth time. Specific to those forty-one pages were the statements of my assailant. His lies were so numerous that I lost count. His words were inconceivable. Yet they believed him and could not "prove" a crime.

How was he so convincing? How was his admittance of sexual assault twice in his statement not taken seriously? He admitted it, but they overlooked it. Was that done on purpose? His words contradicted one another, even within the same paragraph. That shows me right there that they were never interested in solving this crime but in protecting their own.

A liar can only lie so much before his lies start to show the truth. If you look carefully throughout the sentences, you will see. He committed a crime, he admitted it, and he still walks as a free man with his police certification. Perhaps I will let a less-partial party make that determination as I share some of the words of his interview. As hard as it is to find my words in my now-hazy mind, I will attempt to explain my feelings with what he said.

He described her as "kinda quirky" and "quiet". "She was not into sex and not a sexual person." He also described her as being a "little freak" when it came to certain things and that "she liked to play the role of innocent" (during sex). He gave examples of this behavior and stated that in the past she had put a pillow over her head, had gotten into the "fetal position" and had said "No, no, no" when he had sex with her. "She was a little resistant."

He stated that she had given him her home address; however, later stated that he had gotten her address from the agency computer.

> Sticks and stones may break my bones, but words will never hurt me. (Unknown)

They did. His words have wounded me. Deeply. No matter what could be said now, if anything were to be, those hurtful words cannot be taken back. They cannot be forgotten because they are seared into my mind with utter disbelief that they could have even been spoken. They were not words fitly spoken but words carefully crafted to set the suspect free. He committed the crime to my body, yet I am the "little freak" who apparently helped him have unfettered access to my body. Words do hurt, no matter how much a children's rhyme tries to convince us otherwise. He said he would deny it if I ever spoke up.

As this chapter ends, I need to move on, and I know that. Yet I am having such a hard time closing it without justice. How do I move on?

How do I leave such a sensitive place after he has left such a negative and indelible mark on me? The bruises he left on me have faded, but his words never will: "Kinda quirky" and "quiet," "little freak."

How do I rest comfortably and peacefully at night knowing that he will never have to spend even one day paying for his crime? How do I relax knowing that he could potentially have another police career with a different agency because he still holds his certification? How do I ever stop questioning how many other victims there are out there and who may be next for him? Because "we will not be able to charge this person with a crime on the facts we have."

How do I move past the absolute lies of his statement? Besides all his lies, how can I go on knowing that he thinks he never did anything wrong? He denied all of his unfavorable actions. All of them.

How in your right mind is it okay to force someone into any form of sex and then lie about your actions? How was it okay to continue doing something when your victim continuously said no and complained of the intense pain to the point of him asking if I was crying? How did he not think he did wrong when he would have to yank my clothing off after carrying my deadweight body to a room? Why did he continue to tell me of the power he had at the police department, followed by telling me that if I ever spoke, he would deny it?

Why did I keep trying to get away or pull my body in the opposite direction from him? Why did he penetrate harder when he then pulled me back into his grip? Why did he have to pin my arms down to the bed, leaving bruises behind? On what planet is it ever okay to hold a female's head down by her hair while forcing her to perform oral sex as she protested her reluctance and disdain in the matter? How is it not sexual assault when he forcefully penetrates her while she falls in utter agony, coupled with tears, only for him to then go harder? How does a normal mind comprehend that is even remotely okay? She had put a "pillow over her head," had gotten into the "fetal position," and said, "No, no, no," when he had sex with her. That is not okay. That is rape!

He painted a terrible picture of me in his numerous lies because he was trying his best to hide his calculated personality, sexual addiction, and manipulative tactics. He did it at my expense. His physical assault of me was not enough for him. Now he mentally defiled me, too, and destroyed my name as he gave an untrue account of what happened. Yet they still believed him even though he admitted it.

He said he would deny it if I ever talked. I just did not think it would be this bad. He is a man who is good at his game, so I should not be surprised.

Now all I hear and believe about myself is "little freak," "little freak," "little freak," because he certainly convinced everyone that is what I am.

Sticks and stones may break my bones, but his words have forever changed me.

Journal Entry

Fearfully and Wonderfully Made

I recently had a discussion with an FBI agent regarding my case. He looked more like a cowboy than an FBI agent as he was decked out in cowboy everything, even down to his boots and ankle holster. He had a caring demeanor from the moment he stepped through the door. His job was to listen to my story as I poured my heart out to him and then to investigate into the possible corruption within my police agency. He sat patiently and listened to every single word I spoke. Some words protruded with anger. Some with tears. He just sat there listening silently to the heartbreak I experienced as a law enforcement officer by another law enforcement officer.

I explained to him the good, the bad, and the ugly about working within my agency. I wanted to make sure I left nothing out about my experience there. So I spoke, a lot. For about two and a half hours, he listened.

I told him how well I was doing as an officer there. I told him that I was frequently being told by those in charge that I was in the top twentieth percentile of probationary police officers. I explained to him how I received the highest grade of anyone ever within the history of the department for my excellent work on my probationary community policing project. I mentioned to him just how much I loved my job, until the unexpected happened.

I then went into the dark and gruesome details of my experience as a female in a male-dominated work environment. I was sexually assaulted multiple times by a high-ranking supervisor. I was sexually harassed to no end by other male officers, with no concern for my being. Many other females at the agency were too.

I was treated like I was beneath everyone else because I was the only female on my squad. Even though I had previously proven otherwise with my superior work and intellectual legal knowledge, my supervisors would double check my work and redo everything I had already done because they no longer trusted me. I mentioned how I was the only one being singled out and called into the lieutenant's office every shift for perceived mistakes, even if I had done nothing to warrant the meeting. My life was a living hell in my last couple months at the agency. It was so much the opposite from my first many months there. To add salt to the wound, I talked of how my probation was extended because of this nightmare. I was the black sheep of the blue family because of someone else's actions.

I sat on the couch fighting my emotions as I spoke with the agent. His demeanor showed concern for my dilemma. I went on to explain that my life at the agency became a nightmare only when I spoke up about being assaulted. It was only then that everything went south for me.

I also allowed the agent to see another concern in my spirit. A very personal concern. Not only was I raped, but I was also raped as a virgin. I pointed out how my assailant took my virginity and how my spirit was even more broken because of that. What guy would want me now? My virginity was gone, and I was damaged goods. My innocence was taken. I dwelled on the fact that I was no longer pure because someone took what was not theirs to take.

In the moment of explaining my heartbreak about my stolen virginity, the agent broke his silence. He stopped me in midsentence and redirected my thought process with true care and compassion. He blew my socks off in that moment as he explained to me that I was still a virgin. He told me that only I could make the choice on when, where, and who I wanted to give my virginity to. He explained that it was my decision, and that something so precious could not be stolen. He told me that my body was my gift to someone special of my choosing, and rape was never my choice. He carefully reiterated that just because I had been assaulted, which was a stolen lust for my assailant, did not mean that I was not still pure and innocent. Although a wounded one now, I was still a virgin!

After the agent spoke his piece on a painful subject, he then quieted again and allowed me to share the remainder of my story. He would occasionally chime in with a question or statement, but he was genuine in his concern for my story. For me. For most other law enforcement officers, as previously had been proven, would have let me continue without helping to correct my mindset on such a sensitive matter to me. His concern for such a matter lightened my soul and lifted a burden I had been carrying around for months.

I still feel dirty and humiliated because of this incident. I am not sure that will ever change. However, I can now rest assured that my body, spirit, and emotions are mine to give and that nobody can take such a private and personal thing from me. It is mine to give to that special someone of my choosing when I am ready.

Many things were stolen from me as I was repeatedly raped. My self-respect. My dignity. My security but never my virginity, because that is sacred to me. My assailant no longer has a hold on the deepest, most personal aspect of me!

Whether he really was an FBI agent, a cowboy, or even an angel unaware, he reminded me of my priceless value and beauty that no man can ever steal! I am still fearfully and wonderfully made and specially preserved for the man of my dreams!

CHAPTER 9

As I sit here and write, I feel like a hypocrite because my emotions and feelings are going back and forth on the goodness of God regarding trauma. My heart says one thing, and my mind says another because Satan is surely the author of confusion. God is the Father of peace (1 Corinthians 14:33), so why is it so challenging to find that peace when I feel like I need it the most? I guess it is a good thing that God does not base salvation off His *feelings*. It is also a good thing that I am not in charge of the world. God, who knows me the best, still loves me the most, despite my emotions and feelings.

I can sit here and beat myself up for my response to different situations. I can cry. I can punch my pillow. I can cut myself off from the entire world (and I have), but God makes no mistakes, even when it may appear to be the biggest flaw in the world.

Our troubles and trials may hurt. They will make us exceedingly uncomfortable. Our grass will wither. Our flowers will fade, but God's word will stand true forever (Isaiah 40:8). Standing in the balances between heaven and hell is the cross of Jesus Christ.

Sometimes God will allow us to bend in the most uncomfortable ways imaginable. He will let us experience some heart-wrenching situations before He steps in. He allowed Satan to consider His servant Job, because God knew that Job feared Him and would not sin against Him (Job 1). Satan brought his best work against Job. Every trauma and trial anyone could imagine, Job experienced it. Yet never could Satan take his life because God would not allow it, and He alone was in control.

Despite how dark life will get, God will give beauty for ashes. He will give the oil of gladness for mourning. He will provide a garment of praise for the spirit of heaviness. He will rebuild old ruins and former devastations. He will cause rejoicing because God, in all His power, can right the wrongs that life throws at us (Isaiah 61:3).

Because of the many trials I have faced in life, I have wandered away from God. Very similar to the prodigal son, in fact (Luke 15:11–32). I, too, have squandered in reckless living. I have sinned against God and am no longer worthy to be called His child.

But God.

He feels compassion toward His children and will run to us as we start our journey back to Him. He will embrace us and kiss us. He will allow us back into His fold and will supply for all our needs with His greatest riches. He wants to celebrate our return home to Him, but we must take the first step.

What is stopping you from returning home?

God will make a way, even when it looks like there is no way. He is the way, the truth, and the life (John 14:7). Even in our trials, God has not given us a spirit of fear but of power and of love and of a sound mind (2 Timothy 1:7). My mind was vastly damaged when my world was turned upside down. Even when I did not want to believe it, however, God's grace was still sufficient no matter how hard I pushed Him away (2 Corinthians 12:9).

CHAPTER 10

I have begged God many times in my life to deliver me from my *enemies*. He can, and He will when He knows they are not good for your purpose. The problem, therein, lies when we bring those people back into our circle because we were not truly serious about being delivered from them in the first place.

It has been determined that some assault victims will turn toward sexual encounters after a rape occurs and some completely shut down sexually thereafter. Reactions to this specific trauma can vary for each survivor. Neither option is particularly healthy after a sexual assault occurs, but a survivor should not be judged on their reactions to such crime to their body. After the last sexual assault, I *ran wild* sexually. Now not in the literal sense of that expression as I was still very selective, cautious, and ashamed. I did not consistently or continually seek out a bed partner just to have one during that season, but I also did not always say no to some requests when I should have. I still had standards within myself, but I also had this deep hurt that was longing to be filled and fixed somehow. Despite the cultural difference, I wonder if Dinah and Tamar felt the same way and did the same thing?

I did not care who I hurt, which, ironically, just ended up being myself in the long run. I gave my body to different men over the months and years because I was *so* broken. I was longing to find a love that I had never known and that I did not know I craved until after I was deeply wounded. I had this need to be wanted and accepted for who I was and not for the baggage I carried on my shoulders. I was not able to fully accept that someone had callously damaged my body, which caused this shift in my whole life and thought process. I ended up putting myself on a fast track to nowhere. I was on the run from God, so it did not feel that any of this mattered anyway.

After a while of running, God stopped the communication with those men, all at the same time. For one reason or another, all contact ceased quickly—with every one of them. At the time, I did not realize it was God because it just felt like another blow that I was not worthy enough to be loved by anyone. I still feel this way, to an extent.

As hard as I pressed, those men would not return my calls, and I did not know why. I tried my best to keep the relationships alive because I was so desperate to feel longed for and *loved*. While God was trying to deliver me from my own ignorance, I was holding a tight grasp to keep those people in my circle. I was not ready to let them, that life, go.

As I look back today, I can see with a clearer vision that it was God delivering me from my "enemies." Now they were not bad people at all, and I would not actually call them an *enemy*. However, they were not the right people for me because they kept me on my path of wreckage. I despised it at the time, but I am thankful now that God saw fit to pluck me out of the hands of the devil when He did. What I was not able to see back then was that while these men did not truly long for me, God was still longing to be my Savior and my friend. He calls us His friends (John 15:15).

God will never leave us nor forsake us, even when we have left and forsaken Him (Hebrews 13:5). He is a true gentleman and will not force Himself on any of us. He will allow us to try to work out our own salvation with fear and trembling for a time (Philippians 2:12). Yet He will still be waiting patiently nearby for us to come home again. His grace is greater than our sin (Romans 5:20–21).

While I have messed up one thousand times over again because of my onus baggage, God still loves me just as I am. He will not finish molding me and shaping me until He is ready to receive me home in heaven. While I am still not sure how to forgive the God of the universe, or even myself, for the trials I have faced, I am reminded that those trials will not last forever. They will not always feel this way. Life does get better eventually.

God is in love with His children, His beloved creations. He will stop at nothing to try to prove that to us even if it takes Him a thousand times to win us over. God will clear up our clouded vision with His spittle. He will not stop until our sight has been restored, even if it takes more than one attempt for us to see clearly again (Mark 8:22–25).

While this is not necessarily biblically based, I like to think that if God puts a Goliath in front of you, it must be because He believes that there is a David inside of you (1 Samuel 17). It has been said that God gives His hardest battles to His strongest soldiers. Again, that is not biblically based, but the thought is helpful amid a trial.

What if, however, it is really that God creates His strongest soldiers out of life's toughest battles? Would you willingly go through trials if you knew you would come out stronger on the other side? Tribulation works patience (Romans 5:3).

God wants to show us what true peace is, but that can only come from a true surrender. John Piper said, "God is most glorified in us when we are most satisfied in Him." We are no longer a slave to our past, to our sin (Romans 6:6). He sets the captives free, but we seem to keep our own selves in bondage with unforgiveness, anger, hatred, and fear because of our life experiences. We cannot continue to sin and expect grace to abound (Romans 6:1–2).

While I did not think it was possible within my own flesh to count it all joy when I was experiencing my own trauma, it, in fact, was. I should have praised Him in the storm, even when I could not see Him. I started sinking when the waves picked up because I took my eyes off Jesus (Matthew 14:22–33).

I should have been able to rest knowing that God would give the wisdom and patience needed to get to the other side of the trial (James 1:2–3). Trusting God is hard when Satan has subtly convinced you to question God's power, ability, and plan. He is very good at adding more doubt into the scenario. Even Eve was persuaded to question God's trust and authority when Satan slightly twisted her thought process (Genesis 3:1–5). Shame on Satan and all his *clever* atrocities.

CHAPTER 11

It has been said that *time* heals all wounds. I call a bluff on the person who coined that phrase. Time separates us from our past, yes. It creates a distance away from the trauma and makes us forget some of the pain. Yet time really just tends to form a permanent separation between the hurt/trauma and God's redemption because we *choose* not to seek out a real cure. What ultimately heals our wounds is hard work toward healing and forgiveness toward God and ourselves.

> Time doesn't heal. God heals, in time. (Dr. Tony Evans)

True healing may come in layers. When a wound is deep, it causes damage that can extend to several layers below the seeable surface. Perhaps you can only see just the tip of the *iceberg*. The wound looks small and manageable, but under the surface, there is a whole story, a whole life, that needs healing. Healing is a process, one layer at a time.

When we are hurting, people tend to come running toward us with unsolicited, unthoughtful cliché comments. Thoughts such as it *is always the darkest before the sun rises*, and *the teacher is always quiet during the test* tend to grind our gears during and after the fire. While we do not wish to hear these thoughts while we are wallowing in our dilemma, the reality is, it is true. God may stand quietly by when we are in the flames, but He will be in the fire with us (Daniel 3). He may not announce Himself to us in ways that we think He should when we are faced with evil, but He can still bind up the mouth of the lions when we are thrown into the den (Daniel 6). He does not have to reveal His tests to us, but He can create a testimony within us through the trial.

A friend shared this thought many years ago, "We look for the will of God like it is some one-time shot, some grand destiny, or job each of us is determined into when, in fact, the will of God is every minute of every day." Perhaps we were created for one significant thing in this life, but God can also manifest Himself in every minute of every day, even in the most mundane tasks and even when we have a story of trauma. Our names and stories may never be known by the rest of the world like the courageous people in the Bible, but it can make a difference and an impact on the one person God wants to save through our journey.

Actor and comedian Steve Harvey said, "Your career is what you're paid for. Your calling is what you're made for." He went on to say, "You have no idea who God made you to be. But you got to hang in there to find out. You can't give up. It's at your darkest He shows up."

The reality is that we have all been through some form of adversity. Adversity has the power to make us bitter or better, stronger or weaker. If we did not experience trauma and heartache, we would not have a story to share. Our story can impact others. God allows us to experience things to help others. He allowed Jesus to experience the cross because He knew that would impact the world for eternity.

Therein lies the question: Am I willing to share and allow my story, courage, and vulnerability to lead others to the cross? Toward healing? Or am I going to allow my troubles and trials to defeat me? Am I going to continue to harbor an unforgiveness between God and myself for the pain that I think He caused or *let* happen?

Even when our plans fall apart, God's plan can still prevail. If our plan A crumbles like the wall of Jericho, there are still twenty-five more letters in the alphabet where God can create a miracle. Are you willing to try a plan B? Or C? Or D? Are you willing to set aside the weight and every sin that easily besets you? Are you willing to run with patience the race that God has set before you (Hebrews 12:1)?

God desires for you to run the race of life with Him as your head coach. You may pick up some nasty bumps and bruises along the way. It is inevitable because you cannot always see the next play in the playbook. Yet He is the author and finisher of your faith (Hebrews 12:2), and He will lead you to the finish line with a "well done, good and faithful servant" (Matthew 25:21).

Journal Entry

When Your Dream Tries to Kill You

We all have dreams and aspirations for our lives that nobody can talk us out of. It is a dream specific to us. It is the ultimate goal in life that we were created for and must attain for our own satisfaction. It becomes our sole identity and focus in life. It defines who we are and what we will become. Yet what happens when that dream tries to kill or harm you?

My dream was to be a police officer. It was a dream that I worked hard for and fought for a chance to be my whole life. After all, not all women can be cops, right? From my earliest memories, I wanted to be one.

Perhaps not always for my mother, but I was typically on my best behavior as a child. I stayed away from the trouble that lurked about. I steered clear of the sex, drugs, and alcohol that so many other kids were dabbling in. I stayed in church as best as I could to stay on the right track. I did my best to be friends with the local cops because they were my greatest admiration. Besides, it is always better to be a friend than a foe with the local guns and badges.

The day came when I finally got to fulfill my dream. My best friend pinned on my badge, and I was off to the races just as soon as I said "I do" to the deputy chief. I was living and loving the dream.

I guess I may have been existing in a fantasy world because it was all too soon that my dream came crashing down on me and became my greatest nightmare. It came crashing down with a vengeance.

What happens when your dream tries to kill you? Mine sent me into a tailspin in which I have not been able to recover from yet. My dream brought about painful assaults numerous times by another police officer. It locked in an eating disorder that I still struggle with today. It has caused me to harm my own body when I feel out of control, which is all the time these days. My dream put me on depression medications because of the deep wound it caused. It has caused me to contemplate an end to my life because my life does not feel worth it anymore. Even my police agency made and continues to make me feel meaningless with their lack of concern for me.

My dream has almost caused me to lose my faith in God; it is only hanging on by a thread. It has made me feel the deepest loneliness possible. My dream has caused me trust issues because surely, everyone is now out to wound me again. It has caused me to fear in more ways than this innocent little church girl ever knew possible. Yes, my dream has wounded me deeply and even tried to kill me.

Friends and loved ones try to fight for me, but my emotional baggage is just too strong. When I am not trying to push them away on my own, I am pretty sure they think of leaving, anyway, because they can only fight so much.

So what happens when your dream tries to kill you and every good thing about you? Well, I guess we will see where life takes me from here. Maybe some miracle will happen, and it will cause me to fly. I am hoping for a miracle. I guess only time will tell.

Think over your aspirations very carefully. Listen to others who try to steer you in other directions. For they may have insight into your plan that you never dreamed of because you are blinded by your ambitions. Some things in life are not worth the pain in the end. Mine sure was not.

I am still thankful for most law enforcement personnel, the noncorrupt ones anyway. I do not think that will ever change. Yes, I am still very jealous of those who get to wear the badge because in some weird sense, they are still fulfilling my dream. I am not sure why I still have the dream that tried to kill me, but I guess it was born into me many years ago. Looking back, it was not really worth it. If I had not accomplished my dream, I would still be "normal," with no rape baggage to lug around for the rest of my life.

So I guess the question is, would I rather live with regret and the feeling of failure for not going after my dreams in the first place, or would I rather live with possible regret from some hurt and turmoil from accomplishing my life's greatest desire? Ask me again in a few years, and my answer may be different. Perhaps my perspective will gain some new perspective in the meantime.

CHAPTER 12

I have seen a saying that says, "Next time you think you are perfect, try walking on water." That saying cannot be further from the truth and is a blatant misrepresentation of who God is. Peter was not perfect when he walked on water, and it showed when he took his eyes off Jesus (Matthew 14:22–33). The difference is, Peter demonstrated faith in God. Faith does not require perfection.

Satan likes to make the world believe that we are fully undeserving of God's goodness. We are not deserving, and he will not let us forget that. God does not owe us anything. Yet it is because of His grace that He picked us up, wiped off the dirt, and gave us everything.

Throughout my journey, Satan has led me to believe that I do not deserve prayer. He reminds me that I cannot fairly ask anything of God because I struggle to trust God's goodness, plan, love, etc. I still have a hard time with ongoing doubt and fear because my worth has been smeared by the tests and trials of life.

The devil has been successful in convincing me that by praying or requesting prayer, I am merely using God for my own gain. He has been holding my mind captive in this matter by reminding me that my baggage is the reason why God left me. He has convinced me that I cannot return to God's fold because of my actions and feelings about God. Sometimes it feels like Satan has formed a *trauma bond* with my heart, too, because of his lies and deceit. Yet I cannot allow him to have that power over me.

God did not leave me. The enemy captured me and pulled me away from God and has been successful in keeping me away because of the lies he has spread about me and to my broken heart.

God stands at our door and knocks (Revelation 3:20). He reminds us over the noise of life that He has redeemed us and called us His own. He is with us when we pass through the waters. He will not let the rivers (life) overflow us or the flames of life scorch us (Isaiah 43). God wants us to walk out of the darkness and into His marvelous light (1 Peter 2:9) even if our learning style does not quite understand how that is done. God is love (1 John 4), and He said that we are worthy of His love.

Why is it so easy to sin freely, but it is not easy to accept God's grace and love freely? Why is it so easy to accept the negativity about us, but we have such a hard time accepting the beauty within us? God sees His blood-bought children through the cross, through His Son. He looks beyond our baggage and proclaims from the heavens, "This is my beloved Son, in whom I am well pleased" (Matthew 3:17). If God sees us through His Son, then He must love us just as much since we were created in His image (Genesis 1:27).

Just because we may have messed up in the past, perceive that we failed at something, or even been the victim of trauma does not mean that God loves us less or sees us as any less. I have struggled for years with the thought that I am a failure because of past trauma, heartache, sin, stupid mistakes, etc. and that God cannot possibly love me because of that. That I can never get back into His good graces because I continually mess up. That I do not deserve Him because of me. Thankfully, I am not that *powerful.*

But God.

He does not see that. He sees me. He sees what I can be. He loves what He sees because He sees me through His Son and not through my sin.

Satan wants to keep me stuck in the mindset that God cannot love me or forgive me because of how I have felt toward God because of my trauma.

But God.

He sent Jesus to heal the brokenhearted. He sent Him to proclaim liberty to the captives and give sight to the blind (Luke 4:18–19).

When you get tired in the race of life, reach down deep into your soul, and find the courage God has planted inside of you. It has been said that "courage is endurance for just one moment more." (Unknown)

You can do all things through Christ (Philippians 4:13). You can walk out of the graves of life. You can drop your baggage and run home to Jesus. God made up His mind about you long before your first sin, mistake, trauma, heartache, emotion, etc. Cast your cares on Him because He really does care for you (1 Peter 5:7).

Journal Entry

Dwindled Faith

I am struggling to remember my faith because I feel like it has been gone for so long now. I really do not have anybody to blame but myself. I could blame the assailant because that added to the issue, but the truth is that my faith was disappearing long before the rapes happened. It has been slowly dwindling away for years now. I feel like God has dwindled away, too, that He cannot possibly love me anymore.

I feel like I could blame the untimely death of my grandmother, and soon after, my mother, but I am afraid that will not do either. My faith, or lack thereof, is purely my own fault because I did not fight for it. I did not put my part into the relationship. I failed. I am afraid at this time that the prodigal daughter that I have become because of my circumstances and actions cannot be loved by the Almighty God.

At the same time, I am not even sure I am ready to run back to God because my mind is so messed up from everything. I know He is not happy with me or my actions. I have ignored Him and have done my own thing for so long now that He cannot possibly be happy with me. I just hope the nails still don't hurt the hands of Jesus each time I mess up. Because I have messed up. A lot!

My heart breaks. My mind is in such turmoil. My actions are wretched. I am rebellious. All because I started letting my faith slip away years ago. How can God love something like that? Why would He want to anyway? For I do not even love me anymore. Nor do I love this mess that I have become.

Journal Entry

One Year

It has been a year now. One year since the last rape occurred. A year since I had to endure the police (my own team) coming into my apartment to investigate the crime of sexual battery against me, their former police officer. One year since the photographs were taken of the room where the crime happened.

One year since I sat in my living room with law enforcement officials to retell the humiliating encounters. One year since I had to show my shameful, naked, and sore body to the nurse and three other ladies to have that daunting rape kit completed. Talk about shame on top of shame! People gawking over your nude body, looking over every inch for bruises, marks, and foreign DNA. I know they felt bad.

One year since I last lay next to my assailant's gun, paralyzed in fear, as he penetrated each part of my body for his pleasure. One year since I felt intense shame for everything collectively happening all at once.

I would like to say that I have completely overcome this hurdle, but I will always be a rape victim and now a survivor. I will always be a former police officer who was sexually assaulted by a member of my own team. I will always be the female cop who never got justice. No, I do not think I will ever truly get over that, but it is time to move forward now. It is time to stop dwelling on this one chapter of my journey and go forth. One chapter does not define my whole story. It is time to get past all the labels life has placed on me. It is time to use this tragedy for my triumph and some other person's victory too.

I have taken a year to heal or "mope," as my friends and family may call it. While I will be healing from this for the rest of my life, I have decided that I will no longer dwell on my past misfortunes. I will get out of bed each day. I will eventually throw away my depression medications. I will exercise. I will not harm my body. I will feed myself. I will look for a new job and a new dream. I will allow God to do as He pleases with this mess with my willing spirit, because things will not get better unless I allow the change to be made within me first.

Watch out, world. I am on fire. I am dangerous, with the Lord by my side and in my heart. I am wounded, but I am not worthless. I am cracked, but I am not crushed. I am scarred but not suppressed. I am marred, but I am a masterpiece. I am broken, but I am still beautiful. I am fearfully and wonderfully made. I have walked through the valley of the shadow of death, yet God was still by my side. He is my source and my strength. He is my strength when I am weak. He is my shelter in the time of trouble. My scars show that I am a survivor.

This is my year. I will be a source to be reckoned with because God will have the glory for the great things He has done and will continue to do through me.

One year. Three hundred sixty-five days. It can make all the difference in the world.

I wonder what five years will bring, and then ten, and then twenty.

Journal Entry
I Have Decided to Follow Jesus

> I have decided to follow Jesus. I have decided to follow Jesus. I have decided to follow Jesus. No turning back, no turning back! (William J. Reynolds)

In deciding to follow Jesus, He accepts me just as I am and takes my baggage as His own. He picks me up, brushes me off, and shows me His unconditional love. He does not see me as a rape victim. He does not see me as a problem child. He does not notice me as the flawed human being that I am. He sees me through the cross.

Through the cross, I am imperfectly perfect.

He knows the pain on my heart from the many violations I have endured. He has seen just how many times I have been judged from this trauma and by Christians at that. Yet He longs to show me what true love is all about. He knows the turmoil that has rested upon my mind and within my nightmares, yet He desires to give me true peace. He understands the anguish in my heart toward my assailant and the police department. He has seen me fight away this tragic situation and has desired to carry me through the storm. He does not judge my baggage. He simply takes it and places it at the foot of the cross.

It has been a long journey. A very long and dark journey. Although it has felt like it most of the time, God has not left me once. No matter how much I have pulled away from Him, no matter how many times I have flagrantly sinned against Him while trying to find my way. He patiently stayed right by my side with His extended hand calmly waiting for me to reach out and take it. He is the perfect gentleman. He will not force Himself on me like my assailant did. I am convinced that He will not leave me or forsake me either. He knows that I have a love for Him somewhere deep within the rubble of my wounded heart. He waits for me to give Him that wound so He can patch it and restore it like only He can.

God weeps at the atrocities that have happened to me because I am made in the likeness and image of Him. He is angered that His child had to experience something so belittling and demeaning. Yet He is still close by in the darkest of the midnight when I cannot handle life as it is. He has been there on the many days I have stayed in bed because I was afraid to wander from it. He has seen every nightmare. He has heard every cry, every bout with anger. Yet He still loves me as His very own. I am His pride and joy.

Some might ask, well, if your God was so loving, then how could He allow something so terrible to happen to you? I have even blamed Him more times than I can count. But the reality is God did not want that to happen to me. He did not cause it or choose it for me. Because sin is in the world, bad things can and do sometimes happen to good people. So I will choose to see it as God giving His hardest battles to His strongest soldiers.

I have cried out several times throughout this journey, "Why me, God?" Yet perhaps the more appropriate question is, "Why not me?" I was chosen for such a time as this. I was created for greatness, for a purpose bigger than me. I was created to show His glory.

As much as I have hurt in this battle, I must remember that God is still good, and He has not brought me this far just to leave me now. He will use my muddy life for His glory! He was not taken aback by this situation. He knew it was coming from the beginning of time. He also knows just how He will use this situation, too, because He will use it since all things work together for His good. He chose me to illuminate His goodness.

Jesus, who was God in three persons, died for me because He loves me so much! I am His creation. I was carefully handcrafted into the likeness of Him. There is no one like me in the world.

Yet I must remember that He also died for my assaulter too. And for all in my police department. Although He hates what they did to me, God still loves them just as much. He wants me to love them and forgive them again too. He is waiting and willing to extend healing and rest for the weary on this journey, no matter what the baggage they may bring along.

As the old hymn boldly proclaims, "Through many dangers, toils, and snares, I have already come. Tis grace hath brought me safe thus far, and grace will lead me home" (John Newton, "Amazing Grace").

The journey may be difficult. In fact, it absolutely will be. So long as there is sin in this world, there is no avoiding that. It will be a challenge to muddle through some days. Yet in deciding to follow Jesus, He will lead me home. Right back into His arms. Right where I have been all along. Directly where I belong.

Journal Entry

I Had a Dream

It has been many years since the last sexual assault, yet I had a nightmare during the night about the man who inflicted trauma on me. Sometimes that happens. There is no warning. No preparation. Just a dream that I cannot control because I cannot wake myself up out of it.

What did wake me up from it was my alarm. When that happened, a whole flood of crippling emotions came with it. That is what trauma does when you least expect it.

Upon awakening, I immediately jumped into questioning God. He is omnipotent, omniscient, and omnipresent. He is the Creator of all things. The First and the Last; the Beginning and the End. He has the power to make things happen and to make things cease. So why did He choose not to stop the trauma I experienced when it was happening? Why did He allow it to happen repeatedly which ripped away every ounce of my dignity and self-respect? Why did I lose everything, and why did he get to keep everything after his actions?

How am I supposed to be fully okay with a God who did not intervene on my behalf? How do I forgive Him? He is the Author and Finisher of my faith. How am I supposed to move past the fact that He allowed something bad to happen to His child? No, this is not about self-pity. It is about trying to figure out how to cope with this "thorn in my flesh."

I fully understand that my trauma does not compare to some people's trauma. I also know that many people go through heartache and heartbreak as it is a part of life. Yet this very specific life-changing incident happened to me. To my body. One man broke into my body. Without permission. Without apology. Without regret. He stole so much more than he could ever know that I will never be able to get back again. And I never got justice.

I just do not understand why, like Job in the Bible, God allows bad things to happen to those He loves. I guess I will never understand this side of heaven. I will always struggle and question how to fully heal from this. Just as soon as I start making progress, a nightmare happens. A memory flashes through my mind. I am triggered all over again. That is part of trauma.

God, where are you in times like this? Where were you back then? I hate that I am mad at you and that I struggle to forgive you. God, this hurts almost as much as it did five years ago. I just need to feel that I can trust you again. I need to know that you never left me because it certainly feels like you did. I just do not understand any of this.

Yes, this entry is very raw and honest. Yet this is the internal dialogue that happens frequently because I do not understand God's ways or life's traumas. Our ways are not His ways, and His ways are not our ways.

This is the real me. My deepest feelings that I tend to keep hidden for fear of judgment. Yet if we are honest with ourselves, I imagine many of us feel like this some days too. Sadly, it is part of life.

I do not need someone to preach at me or to console me with cliché sayings. I need God to show up in a big way to tell me the He still has a plan for the pain because He does not waste anything. I need to feel enveloped in His love because it has been such a long time since I have felt that. I need to feel believed and validated, not just by the people I am doing life with but by the God of the universe, because I struggle to accept that He actually believes what happened to me. That is the doubt and uneasiness that trauma *brings along with it. I just want to feel safe and loved. By God. By people. I do not desire to be held as a captive in this nightmare any longer.*

I had a nightmare during the night last night. This entry is the final destination from the flood of memories that resulted. Do not judge me. Just love me as I am. A sometimes-lost and wandering soul that just needs to be loved and cherished. Just like all of us in this life.

CHAPTER 13

Hurt people, hurt people. I do not want to end up being that person that someone else must heal from simply because I choose to hold tightly to the pain and baggage of my past. When we choose to stay *stuck* in life, we are simply saying that we do not have a story worth telling. We are stating that we are not worth being healed—but we are. We are worth the hard work it takes to be whole once again.

The Apostle Paul (formerly Saul) *hurt* Christians (1 Corinthians 15:9–10; Acts 8:1–3; Galatians 1:13–23; 1 Timothy 1:13). He persecuted them, killing many in a violent manner simply because they served God. God still showed mercy and grace toward Saul and gave him a miraculous transformation on the road to Damascus (Acts 9). Saul's name then changed to Paul after that transformation. Paul spent the remainder of his life serving God and was used to write much of the New Testament in the Bible.

I wonder what the victims of Saul (Paul) must have thought when he died and entered the gates of heaven. Did their jaws hit the floor when they saw him? Did they forgive him for taking their lives so brutally? Did they happily welcome him into heaven? Did they tremble in fear? Did they question God's motives because of Paul's heinous past? God sent His Son to die for everyone, including the evildoers in this life.

I have spent years being hurt. Years trying to disassociate from the past. Years trying so desperately to understand all of this. Years questioning God on why this happened. Years wondering where the true justice is. I still seem to come up short on finding the answers I crave. Yet I no longer dwell on the name or badge number of my assailant because I am no longer giving him that power over me, that power that has kept me *stuck* for years. I no longer want my hurts to hurt others.

I will not allow the darkness of my past to dim the light for my future. I refuse to let the baggage of my yesterday be the excuse for why I cannot do something great in my tomorrows. If I cannot do something, it is simply because I choose not to try, not because I am not good enough or strong enough to succeed.

The biggest obstacle I will ever face is that of my own mindset. I can either create beauty from the ashes because I choose to fight, or I can make something once beautiful remain as a mere pile of ash because I choose to accept defeat. Obstacle or opportunity? It is my choice.

Bad things do happen to good people. Yet good people can rise above, adapt, and overcome. Beauty is in the eye of the beholder. Success will be found only in those who choose to never give up when life gets hard. What is your mindset today?

I will likely always be the black sheep of the blue family. Yet more than that, I am a child of God's family. Trauma, baggage, and death is swallowed up in victory (1 Corinthians 15:54), and I am no longer a slave to my past. I no longer must hurt others because my hurts have been healed by God. I will never forget the past, and I will always quietly want justice and change, but at least I can proceed on to a brighter future because God has shown me that I am an overcomer.

Life has been consistent in showing me that trials will come. Yet by the grace of God, I am who I am today (1 Corinthians 15:10). Instead of the title of vic*tim*, I am now a vic*tor* in Christ, and you can be, too, because thanks be to God who gave us victory through Jesus (1 Corinthians 15:57).

Sometimes, when we share our story, others look at us and think that we are vying for pity or sympathy. That is not always an accurate or fair assessment of the situation. Healing takes a certain amount of vulnerability. Recognizing that we have a story means that, at some point, we were broken by life. Speaking our journey out loud does not mean that we are still broken or that we are choosing to remain in our brokenness. It simply means that we are finding, or have found, healing, and hopefully others, too, can find healing because of our scars. Victim to victor.

Scars show that we are survivors. While it may be painful and unsightly at times, our scars, our story is a beautiful reminder of just how far out of the wilderness God has brought us. He cares about the little things.

It is okay to let others see the cracks in your armor; that is how the light (Jesus) gets out. Let your scars, your cracks, live out loud today. Others are healing because of the strength and courage within you.

Proclaim victory over your situation. Speak life into the dry bones (Ezekiel 37:1–14). You are stronger than you think.

Today, I will conquer my giants. I will rise up in the face of my enemies. I will be strong. I will be courageous because God will fight for me. I will not fear because He will do great things.

I have waited upon God, and even in the darkest valley, He has renewed my strength. He did not leave me. He did not forsake me. He just patiently stood by and stayed the course for me.

Today, I will run and not be weary. Today, I will walk and not faint. Today, I am laying aside every weight that has so easily beset me because this captive has been set free.

Today, I will not be bitter because of what was. I will be better because of what is to come. I will not let the memory of faded dreams squelch the possibility of new hope for the future. I shall not be dismayed.

With God, I shall do valiantly. I will run with patience the race that is set before me because when the Goliath of life stands in front of me, I know that God has put a David inside of me.

What Satan meant for evil God will use for good. I am confident that the very God who began a good work in me will perform it until He calls me home.

Yes, today I will conquer my giants. I will be anxious for nothing. And whether I fly or whether I fall, I will give thanks because He will be my shield and portion as long as life endures.

While I still do not have all the answers nor did I ever receive justice or an apology, one thing I know is that God has never once approached my situation with doubt in His mind. He does not see me as any less just because I have some unsightly scars. He does not view me as broken and irreparable. He has made me more than a conqueror on this journey, not because I survived everything life has thrown at me but because of His love for and grace toward me (Romans 8:35).

Somewhere along the journey, I lost sight of the fact that God never said that the weapons would *not* be formed against me. They will be formed because we live in a lost and dying world. Yet He promised that they would never prosper (Isaiah 54:17). God is the supreme authority over my life and over anything I could ever walk through. What Satan meant for evil, God will use to strengthen me and uplift me for His ultimate purpose because He never lost sight of me. He never thought of me or saw me as a failure. Yes, the weapons were formed against me, and sometimes I still feel very afraid of them because they can be powerful, controlling, and intimidating. Yet they did not and will not prosper because God has His righteous hand on me. He spoke authority over them. He will bind up the mouth of the *lions* just as He did for Daniel in the Old Testament (Daniel 6). Daniel still had to walk among those lions because it was part of his journey, but God bound up their mouths so they could *not* destroy him.

My issue is no longer my identity. I am no longer identified as the rape victim (survivor). I am no longer seen as the police officer that did not make it in that line of work. As much as I have been made to feel otherwise along the journey, I am *not* the black sheep of the blue family. In fact, when I was the *lost sheep*, the Shepherd (Jesus) left the other ninety-nine sheep just to come and find me because He cared that much for me. He pursued me because He saw my value. When He found me, the lost and wandering sheep that I tend to be at times, He held me in His arms and rejoiced because I was finally home (Luke 15).

I no longer feel angry about the scars I have collected along the journey of life. They are and will always be there because that is the point of a scar. It is a reminder that I survived the difficult times of life. My identity can only be found in Christ, not in my circumstances. I am a blood bought and beloved child of the highest King! The very King that laid down His life for me because He saw something special in *me.* He saw past everything I was and could be and still chose me anyway. He does not hold my past against me. He does not see me as wounded. He sees me as His new creation because He formed every intricate detail about me. He *chose* me. He wants to love and heal you too.

However it is done, forgive God for the things you have suffered from the baggage life has made you carry. Forgive yourself for carrying it for so long. God is not done with you yet, with your story. He has offered you freedom from your chains. If the God of the universe has made you free, you shall be free indeed (John 8:36)!

I often wonder how many times I rob God of blessing *me.* How many times does God want to perform a miracle in me and/ or through my life, but I do not allow Him that opportunity to do so because I lack faith and trust in Him, perhaps because of my past heartaches? God can do things beyond our wildest comprehension, and sometimes He wants to. Yet I tend to forget that God can do the impossible in any situation because He believes *I am possible.*

Whether you are like me and have experienced a trauma behind the badge, there are many out there who have, or whether you have just experienced trauma in general, you matter. Your story matters. You, too, can get through this dark season. Your story can make a difference for someone else if you are willing to be vulnerable in the healing process. God so strongly desires to bind up your wounds. Healing is possible because God believes we are possible.

Your past may be dark, but your future can be bright. You are wounded, but you are not worthless. You are cracked but not crushed. You are scarred but not suppressed. You are marred, but you are a masterpiece. You are broken, but you are beautiful. Be strong and courageous (Deuteronomy 31:6). Fight a good fight, finish the race, and keep the faith because *you matter* to God (2 Timothy 4:7).

You are an overcomer!

EPILOGUE

Dear Assailant,

I have been angry with you for a long time—years, in fact—as you did irreparable damage to my life. I am not even sure you realize just how much heartache your actions have caused me. Yet holding on to the pain of the past does not aid in my healing whatsoever. I have finally come to a place where I need to forgive you so I can finally be free.

It has taken me many years to process and then work through this trauma, yet I did so because I am an overcomer and am worth so much more. In God's eyes, I am His beloved creation that He loves with an everlasting love.

Everything has changed for me now; however, I am choosing to see the good in life because life truly is beautiful, even amid the ashes. I can never forget the past, but I am making a conscious decision to no longer allow my past to lead me or dictate my future. Forgiving you frees me.

I sincerely hope that someday, you, too, can find peace and healing from God and from anyone else you may have hurt along the journey. It is genuinely a remarkable feeling to *know* true freedom. While I no longer dwell on the past, I will remember your name to pray for you each day because God loves you so much.

I have allowed these hurtful deeds to have a mental hold on me for years now because the wound was deep. However, I am taking back my power today in preparation to achieve greater things tomorrow. I was not created to be just another statistic with no name, nor was my story meant to end with being the black sheep of the blue family. I was created for greatness. I will strive to help others with my story.

I guess this is where I should thank you, because I would not have my story without you. I never wanted it, and I would not wish this on anyone else. I will never be able to forget it. Yet, with that, I choose to forgive you for my own peace of mind to help others along my journey.

Sincerely,
Your victim (survivor)

Dear Police Agency,

This letter is not being written to seek retaliation or defame any one person. In fact, it is quite the opposite. It is being written to plead for the desperately needed change within the law enforcement and first responder career field.

Perhaps you see what happened to me and would like to blame either me or my assailant. While his actions against me were his own choices, you played a huge part in his behavior too—by allowing it to happen for years. You did not stop him even after knowing his reputation. You enabled him when you ignored my pleas for help. You allowed him to remain employed, on patrol, and in charge of an entire squad of police officers during the duration of the investigation. You did not afford me the protection I deserved when you found out he was your own officer.

You failed me just as much as he did with each violation. I was expected to fight alone against you and him. Whether you choose to believe it or not, each one of you involved in my story, and in hundreds of other stories across America just like mine, is responsible for what happened to me while I wore your uniform and thereafter. I was not only wounded by my assailant but also by you as well.

You ultimately made the decision to do nothing after I finally had the courage to speak up, even just a little bit. Then, when I finally did speak up, you diminished me and what had happened to me. You showed me that I did not matter despite all my hard work and dedication to your agency.

How will this change for current and future females who step into your agency and wear your uniform? Change is what I so desperately want to see for all the women in the first-responder career field.

Never again do I want to hear that another female officer was sexually harassed or sexually assaulted under your watch because she was ignored. Never do I want to hear that you left her to fight alone in her darkest hours. Never do I want to see that she was then targeted and intimidated by those in control at her agency because she bravely spoke up about the injustice done to her mind, body, and soul, whether it is sexual harassment or sexual assault. Never do I ever want to hear that she was forced to resign or even chose to quit because she could not handle the pressure put on her by you and her perpetrator after she reported the incident.

Hopefully, this never happens again, especially cop on cop. However, if it does, tell her she is brave for coming forward. Afford her the proper respect and privacy she needs to share the intimate details of what happened to her. Allow her to grieve for the piece of her that was forcefully taken from her. Let her cry or scream out in anger, if needed. Help her process what just happened to her because while she may be a first responder, she is also a victim.

Yes, she is a police officer, and she should know the next steps to take. But remember that she is also a human being who has just endured something very difficult. Rightfully so, her mind may not be in the proper place to register and then take the next step. Guide her on what to do next. Do not judge her or make her feel judged because you think you know what happened. Do not allow her to feel alone in her world or on her squad, especially when her life is based around your career field.

She may be hesitant and filled with fear because she is surrounded by men who wear the same uniform as hers and as her perpetrator's. Do not give her the chance to isolate herself because she feels that nobody cares...or worse yet, that nobody believes her. Shower her with the care and concern that you would if that were your own daughter. Get her the proper help she needs. Protect her. Show her you care and that you are on her side every step of the way.

Never blame her. Never minimize or demean her because her assailant already has with the harassment or assault. Fight for her and with her because she deserves it more now than ever before. Her life matters too.

Make it safer for other females to fulfill their dreams of being a law enforcement officer. Set the bar high. Be the change that is so desperately needed within this career field. Live up to your slogan to protect and serve, even those within your own walls.

Female first responders matter. Make a change and be the change for them.

Lastly, I forgive you for your part in my story because forgiving you sets me free.

Sincerely,
Your former officer

While I experienced many tests and trials in law enforcement that I would never wish upon another, I still cherish my time behind the badge. Police officers are still my heroes, and each of their lives matter. I hope I made a positive difference for those I had the privilege of serving. Even now, while I am not in law enforcement any longer, I hope my story will make a difference for others. Despite this trauma, being a police officer has always been my greatest honor.

My Greatest Honor

I'm up before most others,
For a job that must be done.
I work into the hours,
Well after setting sun.

I try to make a difference,
In the moments I possess.
I will fight for simple freedoms,
At anyone's request.

I will walk into the darkened place,
That few would ever roam.
I would sacrifice the life I have,
So, you can make it home.

I will take on all your battles,
Though evil lingers near,
And I will stop at nothing,
To calm your every fear.

I will leave behind my family,
To come and hold yours close.
No matter what the hour,
I'd fight for them the most.

I reach out to the lowest,
The ones that want my life.
I'm prepared to face their struggle,
With every ounce of might.

I don't always see the greatest,
For I'm called in at the worst.
I am there to solve your problems.
I comfort through your hurts.

I will be the face of justice,
Or simply just your friend.
No matter what the moment,
My limits have no end.

I am not always perfect,
But I do the best I can.
I'm here to make a difference,
For the greater good of man.

Many times, throughout my journey,
I have my fears and doubts.
I simply want to make it home,
To those I care about.

I've been kicked and punched and spit upon,
Cast to the lowest shame,
I've been scorned and mocked and ridiculed,
I've been called so many names.

I rarely hear a thank-you,
Or just a word of care.
But just the time you need me,
I will certainly be there.

Sometimes I go home weeping,
The tears I can't control.
The issues I've encountered,
Have reached into my soul.

This is the life I've chosen,
Yet, my job, it must be done.
So boldly will I press on
Until my race is run.

And should I fall in battle,
And wane with fleeting breath,
Don't stand by and weep for me,
As I close my eyes in death.

For this journey that I'm called to,
Though at times might seem quite dim,
It has been my greatest honor,
And I would do it all again.

ABOUT THE AUTHOR

While Olive Elise did not get to spend much time in her dream career of law enforcement, she was, at least, given the opportunity to accomplish her childhood dream of becoming a police officer. While it did not work out for her in the end, she has always believed that she made a difference during her time in that career field. Olive Elise now believes God is going to use her story to help others heal from their own scars. Never lose hope in a big God and a brighter tomorrow!

Olive Elise makes her home in the Eastern Standard time zone with her very spoiled furry companion.

9 798891 120327

Printed by Libri Plureos GmbH in Hamburg,
Germany